ONE HABI

Ashdin Doctor is The Habit Coach™. He firmly believes that an awesome life starts with awesome habits.

He hosts The Habit Coach™ Podcast on IVM, which is a daily podcast that has over a thousand episodes. It is ranked among the top self-development podcasts in India. It covers a wide variety of topics all designed to help the listener evolve through their daily habits.

He works with people from all across the world, helping them with their habits, spreading his message through key note speeches, workshops and group coaching sessions. Apart from that, he is a director at Ormax Consultants Pvt. Ltd., Ormax Media Pvt. Ltd. and Ormax Evolve Pvt. Ltd. He is also a trustee at the Light of Life Trust, an NGO dedicated to underprivileged children around the world. Ashdin will be donating a percentage of the proceeds from this book to the NGO to promote literacy.

BASED ON THE POPULAR IVM PODCAST, THE HABIT COACH™

ASHDIN DOCTOR

ONE HABIT A DAY

31 Habits to Transform Your Life

Published by Westland Books, a division of Nasadiya Technologies Private Limited, in 2023

No. 269/2B, First Floor, 'Irai Arul', Vimalraj Street, Nethaji Nagar, Alapakkam Main Road, Maduravoyal, Chennai 600095

Westland and the Westland logo are the trademarks of Nasadiya Technologies Private Limited, or its affiliates.

ISBN: 9789395767149

15 14 13 12 11 10 9 8

Typeset by Jojy Philip, New Delhi

Printed at Thomson Press (India) Ltd

Contents

Judge No More

Have you heard of Ur-Nammu? He was the founder of a Sumerian dynasty in the ancient city of Ur. He was also one of the earliest known legislators. Around 4,000 years ago, in 2200 BCE, he formulated an elegant system of law based on cause and effect. The code of Ur-Nammu goes like this: If a man commits murder, then he must be killed. If a man commits robbery, then he must be killed. You get the drift.

There is a whole list of these laws you can find online. Written on clay tablets and preserved, the code of Ur-Nammu makes for entertaining reading centuries later. The laws are all about slave ownership and virgin wives. In today's times, these things are quite unthinkable. Yet, people did live by these laws back then, at least in the city of Ur.

Laws provide a framework for good conduct. Ur-Nammu would have laid down these laws to encourage a moral way of living. But following them today would be blasphemy. Our judicial system has evolved much since then. Our laws are more complex. We have a judge who presides over the judiciary system. There are multiple layers to protect the various rights enjoyed by people.

We think of the system we have now as being better than what existed earlier. But, 4,000 years from now, the same system might be thought of as savage and inhumane. This is because the definitions of right and wrong are not static; they are constantly changing. As society changes, so do morals and rules. With time, the idea of what is acceptable evolves.

The problem arises when we start believing what we consider right to be the absolute, unchanging truth. As soon as we define a particular way of doing something as the only right way of doing it, everything else automatically becomes wrong. However, as we have just seen, there is no such thing as right. It is all relative.

When we start classifying things as right and wrong, or good and bad, we are judging them. And it is this judgement that creates all kinds of problems in our lives. We begin to stereotype people. We distance ourselves from them and build walls based on arbitrary ideas of right and wrong.

If you look at the problems in today's society, you will notice we are constantly alienating people and creating rifts. We judge people for what they eat, wear or speak. And we are so quick to judge that we often don't bother to find out their whole story.

When we judge others so swiftly, an important aspect of being human disappears: tolerance, which is our ability to acknowledge others and their points of view, even if we don't accept them. When we judge, we lose the ability to acknowledge difference. We simply dismiss alternative ways of thinking and being. Instead of instantly judging, imagine if we could, for a brief moment at least, look at things from another perspective.

As your habit coach, I want you to change your mindset from judging to learning. Instead of passing judgement and dismissing something you don't agree with, try to see what you can absorb and learn from it. Move away from seeing things in terms of absolutes and make room for different perspectives.

This is a powerful habit to create because it is a habit of learning and so a growth habit. In comparison, the habit of judging stunts our mind.

The other day, I was spending a night at the farm. I was sitting and peacefully looking at the stars. Suddenly, from across the river, came loud music and the noisiness of people having a really good time. My first reaction was irritation. *Look at those idiots, ruining the lovely peaceful atmosphere* I thought. But I instantly checked myself. It wasn't necessary that everyone enjoy nature the same way that I do. They had decided to let loose and party, something I hadn't done in a while. I reminded myself of the thrill of masti with friends and immediately felt calmer. This is a small example of how you can consciously develop the habit of non-judgement.

The snap judgement will happen, you just have to recognise and undo it. So, whenever you catch yourself judging something or someone, pause and ask yourself: *What can I learn from this? Is there a new way of seeing the world? Is there a new idea here?*

Don't think in terms of right or wrong, good or bad. That is irrelevant. What is good today might be bad tomorrow. It is fluid, there is no absolute truth.

In the end, notice how throughout this chapter, not once did I say judgement is wrong or bad. I didn't judge judgement. Instead, I just offered you a new perspective.

Exercise

The next time when you come across someone who is different from you, observe your thoughts. Are you judging them as right or wrong?

If so, let us practise tolerance.

Try to look at the same thing from a different perspective and write down two reasons why you can acknowledge their viewpoint.

_____

_____

_____

Now, write down two things that you can learn by acknowledging their point even though your own point of view is different.

_____

_____

_____

Practise this in your day-to-day interactions and you will soon realise that placing people in buckets of right/ wrong/ good/ bad is unnecessary. The more you are open to learning, the more fluid your viewpoints will be.

The Habit of Happiness

Did you know, the word 'happy' comes from the Norse word 'hap', meaning luck or chance? Similarly, 'bonheur', the French word for happiness, comes from 'heur'. It, too, means luck or chance. The German word 'glück' has the same meaning—luck and happiness intertwined. By now, you may be wondering if this implies that happiness is not a constant but comes by chance—or haphazardly (see what I did there?).

So, does this mean happiness is not in our hands? Can we only be happy if we're lucky? Can the two exist without each other—luck without happiness or happiness without luck? Or are we only lucky when we are happy? Is life filled with so many uncertainties that we need luck on our side to be happy?

I am sure that was the case centuries ago, when villages were ravaged by war and famines. Maybe happiness was only found by people when luck favoured them. We are lucky that we have far fewer hardships and challenges in modern times.

However, I refuse to believe that luck has a lot to do with happiness. Happiness is something we should all be working towards. It is something we should have as a goal and a mission.

The idea I want to drive home is that 'happiness' itself should be a fundamental habit of ours. Imagine being focused on making happiness a habit, whereby we consciously dedicate time and energy towards cultivating it!

What the definitions mentioned earlier do state is that happiness is not a natural state of being. No one is happy all the time and we can see this with everyone we meet. Our default setting is that of negativity, indifference, sadness or fear. Seeing someone happy for no reason is confusing.

Try an experiment: walk around your office smiling. I bet people will stop you and ask what you are so happy about. That's because it is a rare thing! Imagine if happiness was our default and displays of sadness, stress or negativity were considered rare and weird. Wouldn't that be something?

Now imagine what your life would look like if you were in a state of chronic happiness. Living with peace, joy, gratitude and positivity. I want you to believe that such a thing is possible.

The main roadblock we face towards practising happiness is the fact that we have no control over our negative thoughts and beliefs. Think about how many such thoughts race through our mind each day.

Something good happens to us and yet, after the initial feeling of joy, we immediately worry about things that could go wrong. We worry that someone will snatch our good fortune away. We worry that things will get jinxed!

Often, we are sad simply because we don't have what someone else does. We are constantly comparing ourselves to other people.

The weird thing is that all of us have a default sadness script that we keep playing in our heads. It could be about loneliness, unworthiness, unfairness, lack of love or something more tangible, like weight or money.

As your habit coach, I want to tell you that it is important that you know what your default script is. Only when we identify the thoughts that are keeping us from happiness, can we begin to do something about it. Awareness of your negative or sad thoughts is the first step to cultivating a habit of happiness.

The next step is to plant the positive thoughts every time you catch yourself having a negative thought. Keep a list of positive ideas and thoughts ready. Wake up every morning and, before you start worrying about all those unfinished tasks you need to get to, give yourself a minute to say, 'I believe today will be a great day.' It doesn't matter if you feel it yet, that will happen with time. If you believe happiness is a habit you must diligently practise it.

You could modify the line according to your default negative script. Remember, that's what we are trying to counter. If you feel inadequate, say to yourself, 'I know I am enough.' If you feel someone has something you desire, tell yourself, 'I am happy for them and I believe I can have it too.'

Turn sad, self-piteous, negative situations around by countering them with ready positive thoughts. If you stumble, remember, often being grateful for something is the superpower that will help you get into the right phase by turning your thoughts towards positivity.

Will this solve all your problems? Of course not. If you are clinically depressed, will practising happiness make you suddenly happy? No, it won't. What it will do is set the foundation for happiness and happy thoughts. It will catch and remove certain negative thoughts from your life. It will allow for a better grasp on your emotions, and, if done for long enough, will become a subconscious habit. Your days will start and feel better. There will be a spring in your step and twinkle in your eye!

So, the two simple steps to start making happiness a daily habit are to catch your negative or sad thoughts and put a positive or happy spin on them. You may have to force yourself initially but keep doing this till it becomes your default mode. Continue telling yourself, 'Life is amazing', 'Today will be awesome', 'I am going to kick ass', 'We are going to have so much fun', 'I will crush this exam.'

In the beginning, it may feel silly. Your negative thoughts may overpower your mind at times. You will wonder why you are doing this. It might even be very hard to think positive thoughts. But I want you to just practise and go through the motions.

Ultimately the best kind of luck is the kind that you create. And, if happiness and luck are so intertwined, we might as well try and create happiness too!

Exercise

Write down three negative or sad thoughts that you frequently have during the course of your day.

_____

_____

_____

Now write down the three thoughts that you can use to replace your negative thoughts.

_____

_____

_____

Every time you catch yourself sliding into one of your default thought patterns from the script, stop and consciously replace it with its corresponding positive thought.

Like everything new, this may feel uncomfortable in the beginning. The more you practise, the easier it will be to catch your negative thoughts in time and replace them with happy ones! Seeding a positive thought will become your second nature. Soon, you wouldn't have to depend on luck at all!

Garden Your Mind

Long-drawn wars are a big strain on the countries engaged in them. Rationing and food stamps are a very big part of everyday life during wars. The Second World War was no different. During this time, the American government found it difficult to produce enough food to feed all its people. A lot of food had to be sent to the frontlines for the troops, and the remaining was rationed out among the people.

To meet this food shortage, the government promoted the concept of victory gardens. Civilians were encouraged to grow fruits, vegetables and herbs to supplement the food stamps they were given. The idea caught on. People used whatever piece of land they could find, be it backyards, public gardens, tops of buildings, and so on. One of the most famous propaganda ads of the time was 'Digging for Victory'.

I first heard about victory gardens when I was researching the Second World War for a project at work. I absolutely loved the idea. Each person, by being responsible for their food, was helping their country fight the war. Planting a victory garden gave them a purpose. It made them feel they were helping the soldiers on the battlefield and contributing towards their country emerging victorious.

I also realised a simple truth. Those who tended their own gardens would be better fed and their life would be easier even during tough times. Those who did not tend their gardens, however, would have less food and, consequentially, suffer.

This is as applicable for our mind, which is like a garden. We are responsible for its growth and the fruits it gives us. Almost all aspects of gardening can be correlated to the way we treat our mind.

If a garden is not tended to, the weeds often take over. In the context of our mental garden, negative thoughts are the weeds. They steal the nutrition that the positive thoughts need to grow. Just as weeds multiply far faster than the plants we intend to grow, so do our negative thoughts if we leave them unchecked.

As any experienced gardener knows, weeds need to be removed on a regular basis. This can be the first step towards cultivating our mental garden. Remove the 'weeds', the negative thoughts that take up space in our mind and share the nourishment ideally meant for good plants or positive thoughts.

Now that you have removed the weeds, the next step is deciding what kind of seeds to plant. Seeds can be likened to the ideas or intentions we have. They need to be chosen before planting. We can't plant orange seeds and then, five years later, expect apples. We have to plant the seeds that will give us the fruit we want. So, how do you find the right seeds, the best quality ones? The best way to get a variety of 'seeds' for your mind garden is to read, listen to inspirational people, and explore new concepts and ideas.

As your habit coach, I think of each chapter in this book, as well as each podcast, article, video and post I've produced, as quality seeds that you can plant in your mind. I take this job very seriously. Your mind garden might not bear fruits for a while, but as long as you choose the right seeds to plant, it is possible for you to have a beautiful and nourishing garden.

Now that you have planted the right seeds, it is important that they receive the appropriate care to fruit and flower. Our everyday thoughts are what we use to water our mind garden—the thoughts that float in our mind all day long. Are you consciously watering your seeds with nurturing thoughts? Or are you overwatering them with too many thoughts and obsessions? Or are you planting seeds and then forgetting to water them, like that one plant in our home that we neglect till it withers.

Introspecting and planning your day are great ways to water your seeds just the right amount. You ensure just enough attention for them to grow—not too much, not too little. The right thoughts can nourish the garden. Obsessive thoughts, on the other hand, will destroy it!

If we want our mind garden to flourish, we have to give it the right fertiliser. This is the knowledge that we get from reading and learning new things about life. Being in a constant state of learning is a great way to grow faster. It feeds the right nutrients to your mind garden. Adding rich, good quality fertilisers is essential to cultivating the garden of your dreams.

Now that our mind garden is in full bloom, what do we do about the pests? Because just like in any organic garden, there will be pests—insects, bugs and animals that destroy and eat up our beautiful produce. We all know people who eat up our heads. They take from us without giving back. They chew on our dreams. They meddle with and mess up the things we are working hard on. They are the pests of our mind garden.

If we use pesticides, or negative feelings of anger or revenge, to deal with them, they may go away, but it would leave us toxic as well. Instead, we have to do what organic farmers do—grow plants that repel them. These are ideas that the pests find unappetising and don't come around for. It could be showing empathy for someone they want you to gossip about or simply setting boundaries that the pest knows not to cross.

Whichever route you choose, make sure to keep the pests out of your garden, the one you are working so hard to create.

The last thing you need for your mind garden is patience. As any gardener will tell you, trees don't grow overnight. Plants will flower only when the season is right. Fruits will appear when it is time. Pick them too early and they are useless. Pick them too late and they are rotten. Patience is the key to growing your mind garden.

Fall in love with the process of gardening. Tend to your mind garden lovingly and it will grow and bloom.

So, your simple habit for having the kind of mind you want is to start tending to it. Treat your mind like a beautiful garden that you are growing. Left unattended it will be useless and unattractive. Weed it, seed it, water it, fertilise it, get rid of the pests and then wait. Patience.

Much like the victory gardens from the Second World War, our mind gardens are the key to the victory of our lives.

Exercise

Find a quiet place and sit comfortably. Put away your mobile phone or any other distractions for a few minutes.

Visualise the garden of your mind.

Now, you first need to remove the weeds (the negative thoughts). At different times of the day, observe your thoughts. Write down three of these negative thoughts and visualise yourself pulling them out of your garden and throwing them away. They do not belong in your garden anymore.

Now, it is time to plant the seeds. What are some of the fruits that you would like to see in the future? These are your goals, intentions, hobbies and ideas. Think carefully and write down two that resonate with you the most.

These seeds need the right amount of water. So, you need to work on your goal daily. Focus on it. Work on it consistently. Track your habits and consistency with a tracker.

Allocate a minimum of 30 minutes towards learning and reading. This is the fertiliser of your mind. Write down some of the books and resources you will learn from.

_____

_____

Protect your garden. Beware of people who are like pests, who discourage your goals. Guard your goals. Write down how you will protect your garden and from whom.

_____

_____

_____

Finally, be patient and keep doing the work. When the right season comes, the trees will flower and then bear fruit.

Anger is Useless

Did you know, there is no one hormone that causes us to get angry? This makes anger a complex emotion. When we think of anger we think of people in a rage. People throwing things. Shouting at the top of their voice. Not being able to calm down. Causing damage to themselves and all around.

In a word, anger, if not controlled, is destructive. It burns and destroys. I get requested for a podcast on anger almost every week. I realise that it is a very common problem. Anger, after all, is an outburst of emotions. We live in a world where there is hardly any emphasis put on emotions. We are not taught how to understand our feelings. In the absence of awareness about how to deal with varied emotions, anger becomes the default.

Think about it. When was the last time you were angry? What was going through your mind? What were you thinking about? Had someone done something to you? Had you done something?

At its most basic level, anger is our response to a stimulus— something that has happened on the outside, in our environment; something that does not fulfil our expectations.

The key thing to remember is that while a situation may anger us, not everyone will react to it with anger. Clearly then, it is not just the situation that is at fault.

Most angry people fall into two categories: those who have no control over their anger and let it consume them, and those who give in to their anger and explode with it.

Then there are people who have, over time, bottled and repressed their emotions to such an extent that they have buried all emotional responses deep inside themselves. These categories are all unhealthy! Do you fall into any of these?

Let's talk about people who have no control over their anger.

Without the right tools, there is no way to control anger. The first stage is to recognise that you're letting anger get into the driver's seat and giving it control over your behaviour. Only when you have calmed down can you get your anger out of the driver's seat long enough to have a moment of introspection. I call this stage the post mortem. Because this happens when the anger has finished destroying you.

So, once you are calm, I want you to analyse what happened. What is it that got you so mad? How is it that you lost all control of yourself? What was it that triggered you so much? What did you do? What could you have done differently?

Then, I want you to name the actual emotion that led to your outburst. It could be fear, desire, jealousy, disappointment, surprise or a feeling of inferiority. The list is long and because we currently don't have the vocabulary to describe all that we are feeling we label it as anger.

One of the best things you can do is print out a list of emotions. It is called an 'emotions chart' and you can easily find one online. When you can name the different emotions, you will be able to point them out and say exactly how you are feeling. This stage is critical and will help you deal with anger the moment you feel it.

Now, let's come to the first step for when you feel anger bubbling within. I want you to take five deep breaths. Yes, that's right. Nothing complicated and fancy. Just deep breaths.

Next, while breathing I want you to focus on naming the emotion that you are feeling. Are you hurt or betrayed? Could you possibly be hungry? Don't we all know people who get hangry? You'll realise that as soon as you name the real emotion behind it, the anger goes away. This is because now the mind has the right vocabulary to understand the situation and deal with it.

For the final step, I want you to use the learnings you collected from your post mortems. How can you deal with a situation that angers you differently? Will anger do any good or will it only give vent to your frustration? Will it help you communicate effectively? Should you leave or fight?

Each person has a different trigger for anger and a different way to express it too. When it comes to controlling anger, there is no one-size-fits-all approach.

What I have given you is a template. I have used it with my clients during habit coaching, to help them with their anger issues. This has greatly helped their relationships.

Some of my CEO clients would lose their cool in the boardroom, throw things around and curse at their staff. After using these techniques, they were able to control this behaviour. As your habit coach, I want you to realise that anger is useless if not channelled properly. It is destructive.

However, if you understand where your anger is coming from, and what emotions are actually behind it, it can help you understand yourself better.

Developing a simple habit can change how you deal with anger—start doing a post mortem on what happened when you were angry.

Follow the steps I mentioned and put yourself back in the driver's seat. Don't let anger be the one in control.

Exercise

For this exercise, there is a preliminary step 0 and then steps one to three.

The preliminary step of this exercise is to find an 'emotions chart' online and take a printout.

Whenever you get angry, wait for it to pass. Let the anger subside. After your anger subsides, think and write down what was the emotion that led to it.

If you were to do it again, what would you do differently? Do this post mortem for a few minutes.

Now that you have done the preliminary step, move on to step one. Whenever you observe anger starting to bubble inside you, take deep breaths—short inhalation and longer exhalation. This will centre you and stop your train of angry thoughts.

Step two is to notice the emotion that you are feeling. Write it down below.

What is the emotion that is making you furious? If there are more one, write them down.

Step three is where you use the knowledge you've gained from all the steps before this one. Decide what is the best course of action and why.

You can choose to communicate your stand assertively. You can choose to fight for what you believe or, if you want to excuse yourself from the surroundings and situation, you can leave.

Whatever you do, you will know that you are choosing to do it. A cool-headed choice and not one made in anger.

_____

Use this template and take control of your life!

_____

A Rewired, More Positive You

Did you know that it is possible to rewire our brains with just the use of positive thoughts?

For the longest time, it was believed that the human brain, once formed, stays the same. We cannot grow or rewire it. However, scientists are now looking at things that help the brain grow and change. One of them is exercise and physical activity. Another, interestingly, is having positive thoughts.

In the book, *The Brain That Changes Itself*, Dr Norman Doidge writes about 'positivity workouts' that can rewire the brain and change old negative thought patterns. Isn't that brilliant? Very often we grow up with people who are negative or have had negative experiences. Sometimes, these become our default thinking patterns. What a relief to know that we can change these thinking patterns even if we can't always control our experiences.

Let us start by understanding what positivity means. The dictionary is useless here because it just says that positivity is the character of being positive. Duh!

For me, positivity is a function of hope that is grounded in reality. Simply put, it means being optimistic about the happenings around us—not jumping to the worst possible conclusions, not seeing things as good or bad, but believing that things can be better. Hope, therefore, is an essential ingredient of positivity. Positivity is the belief that the present is amazing and the future is going to be even better.

So, how do we cultivate positivity? First, it is imperative that we reduce the negative load in our lives. The people we spend time with, the news we read, the shows we watch and so on must not be overtly negative. When we expel the negative from our lives, we can add positive things instead. We must seek out and surround ourselves with positive icons, positive stories, positive memes.

Then, we need to challenge ourselves to see hope and goodness in everything around us, especially in those we cannot change. Let me share with you how I have actively brought positivity into my life.

Step 1: I stopped listening to the news unless it was something funny on a late-night show or from a positive news outlet. If the news was important, someone would end up telling me about it. Then, I slowly stopped interacting with the negative people in my life or started coaching them to get out of their negative loops. On social media, I unfollowed people who were always being negative.

Step 2: I created an environment of positivity around me. I associate Superman with strength and positivity. So, I have a Superman mug, a Superman keychain and a Superman mobile cover. In my office, I even have a Superman carpet. People might wonder if I'm trying to turn into Superman, but it's the symbolism I am tapping into. I also have a deck of affirmation cards that I keep in my den and read from time to time. When friends come over, they pick a card and see something fun and positive written on it. My desk is full of post-it notes with my goals scribbled on them. When people ask me, 'How are you doing?' I reply by saying 'Rocking!' And you know what? I mean it too.

These are my ways of cultivating positivity in my daily life. Your methods may be entirely different. It doesn't have to be Superman. Maybe reading about acts of kindness around the world sparks positivity in you, or watching puppy videos. You need to find something small that is easy to do and requires little effort. Something that works on a subconscious level and creates a sense of positivity in you.

As your habit coach, I want you to work on these two steps. Remove the negative and add lots of positive things around yourself. The chapter titled 'Garden your Mind' on page 12 will help you develop this idea further.

Your super simple habit of being more positive starts with creating an environment of positivity around you. Begin by seeing where you spend the most part of your day, and the changes you can make there to bring about more positivity.

Make five positive changes around you. It could be anywhere— your office, home, car or accessories. Maybe, unicorns are your symbol of positivity! I am curious about these changes you make. Take a picture and share it with me on my Instagram account (@Ashdindoc). Add the hashtag #OneHabitADay

Small changes slowly rewire the brain to look for positivity everywhere. That is what we want to achieve. That is our holy grail. I know that you are someone who wants positivity in their life. That is why you are here reading these words. Let's make positivity a habit that grows and grows!

Exercise

1. Now that you have made space for positivity in your life, think of a symbol that reminds you to be positive. It can be the peace sign, a favourite animal, or a ... unicorn! Surround yourself with the symbol of your choosing in different forms. Every time you see it, think of what it represents to you, and draw positivity from it.

2. Keep flashcards of affirmations and quotes that fill your mind with positivity. Write three of these quotes or affirmations below.

   ----

3. Reframe your vocabulary. Write a list of five negative words that you use. Now, work on a list of five positive words that you can and will use instead.

Being Grateful is Great for You

Practising gratitude has proven to be the most transformative habit in my life. If there is only one habit you pick up from this book, please make it gratitude. I know it will be the most powerful tool for you.

Did you know that gratitude can improve the quality of your health? There are studies that indicate that people who approach life with a more grateful demeanour have a better quality of life and health.

The number of things that gratitude can help us with is unbelievable. A simple search on the internet will leave you bombarded with things like, 'Thirty-one ways in which gratitude can change your life', 'Seven benefits of gratitude on your health', 'Improve your social life with the attitude of gratitude' and 'Sleep better with a gratitude practice'.

The list is endless.

My gratitude practice started when I had come out of a very bad stage in my life. A toxic relationship had ended, I had moved houses and was restarting my life almost from scratch. My self-esteem was low, my future was uncertain and the life I had known thus far lay shattered in a thousand pieces. I was scared. Fear was the main emotion of my existence.

You see, when you are living a life of fear, it is very hard to see the positive in anything. You feel that the world is against you. Self-pity is your constant companion. Why me? How could life be so cruel? These kinds of questions often make their way into your thoughts.

You take everything in your life for granted. You feel entitled. This is because you are so focused on yourself that you can't see the good in others. You feel you are entitled to all the good that happens to you because of all the bad things that have happened to you in the past. Entitlement is the opposite of gratitude.

You lay awake at night fighting to keep the worrisome thoughts at bay: the stressful job with the mean boss, the financial problems that keep chasing you, your need to juggle home and work and everything in between. You want to hide from the things that bother you, so you go out every night to blow off some steam and party into the wee hours. All this to forget what you are running away from.

This was my life. I would go out, party all night and crash at four or five every morning. Now, I get up at five every morning. I compare my past life to the one I lead now and cannot help but marvel at the change.

It was at that lowest point in my life that I started my gratitude practice. I had lost all hope. Yet, I would wake up in the morning and force myself to think of three things to be grateful for. I would then write them down in a journal. The first week of this practice was hard, but by the second week, I was smiling every time I wrote something down to be grateful for.

Within a month of this gratitude practice, my life changed. This could happen because my mindset had changed. I was unrecognisable. The fear was gone. The worry was gone. I was a different person.

Gratitude is the feeling of thankfulness for something, someone or some event. It is appreciating someone for the impact they have had on your life. It could be the smallest things, like someone holding a door open for you or sharing their food with you. Gratitude enables us to be mindful of the many things people do for us without asking for anything in return.

The word gratitude evokes a feeling. This feeling supercharges the brain with a cocktail of chemicals. It is built into our biology. As human beings are social animals, we have evolved to live together and do things for each other. Our social system would break down if this stopped.

You can actually see that happen the world over. As we grow into a 'global' society, where the world is only a few clicks away, we are becoming more individualistic and less social. It is in times like these that gratitude is necessary.

Here is how you begin to work on your gratitude practice. Start by writing down three things you are grateful for. Write out full sentences. 'I am grateful for my mother and her unconditional love for me.' You can give a reason for the gratitude you feel, if you like, but it is not necessary.

The real power comes next. For the next thirty days do not repeat a single thing on your gratitude list. This means by the end of it, you will have ninety separate things that you are grateful for. When I tell this to my clients, they don't believe me at first! It feels impossible to think of ninety things in one go. But when you get down to it, you remember that Hindi teacher in school who showed you so much kindness, that birthday party that was so special and your favourite cricket bat that went with you everywhere.

Slowly, you begin to realise that life has been good to you. Even through the bad times, there have been moments of joy. Simply put, there have always been things that you can feel grateful for.

So, your super simple habit starts by getting a notebook and a pen. No, do not do this on your mobile phone or computer. It works better if you write it down, trust me.

Practise this habit every morning with your tea or coffee. Find a particular spot where you won't be disturbed. Spend at least fifteen seconds visualising and focusing on the thing you are grateful for. Let that emotion run through your mind.

Be ready for your life to change.

Exercise

Write down three things that you are grateful for. It can be about a person who has helped you or a thing you recently bought or even an incident that made you happy. It can be the smallest of joys.

I am grateful for _____

_____

_____

_____

Now visualise each of these things. Spend a few seconds recollecting the memory. Allow yourself to feel the gratitude anew.

Do the same exercise daily for the next 30 days, following the two rules below.

1) The sentence must start with 'I am grateful for...'

2) There can be no repetition in these 30 days. Find new things to be grateful for.

_____

As you write and visualise, you will start to see your life changing in front of you. Behold the magic of gratitude unfold!

_____

Push the Pull Door

Did you know that January was named after the god of doors? Did you know that there is even a god of doors? This is why I love researching fun facts.

January is named after Janus, the Roman god of doors or archways. In ancient Rome, doors did not just serve a utilitarian purpose, they were also used as symbols of power. Imposing free-standing doorways were built. Roman armies would pass through these great big structures to go to battle. Notice how even today we have so many symbolic free-standing doors. The Gateway of India in Mumbai, the India Gate in Delhi and the Arc de Triomphe in Paris are all gates that represent much more than just a doorway.

Janus is also the god of new beginnings, which is why he is associated with doors. Think about how we welcome a new bride home. It's through a small ceremony performed at the door. In some cultures, brides are carried over the threshold, symbolising the transition into a new life.

We don't realise it, but many things we do unthinkingly today have deeper meanings tied to them from the past.

In ancient Rome, for instance, the way someone opened a door symbolised how well they had served Rome. Only those who had helped expand the empire would have the honour of a door that opened outwards.

Nowadays we just stick a sign that says 'pull' or 'push' on a door according to our convenience. All the symbolism is lost, replaced with an instruction. But have you noticed, some of the doors that instruct you to pull, can also work perfectly fine if pushed and vice versa? When I was a kid, pull and push stickers were very popular on doors. They used to be a great source of amusement to us kids, especially if they confused people.

We had a family friend who played an influential role in my life—Phiroze Engineer. He was a lovely man, an independent thinker and an entrepreneur. I remember an incident with him so vividly. He was telling my parents, 'I always pull a door that says "push" and push a door that says "pull". As a kid, I found it funny, but also strangely profound. Today, so many years later, it is something that has remained with me, leading me to believe there was more to Phiroze's statement than was apparent. That one line of his has many layers to it. Through it, Phiroze is making a case for independent thinking.

When you blindly follow what someone says, you are not thinking for yourself. You are not using your brain, you are simply following the herd. The herd is safe but there is no room to grow as an individual. It is important for us to break away from the herd, from time to time.

The other thing I learnt from Phiroze's simple statement is that one must question everything. Why should you believe what someone else is saying? Question it! Why should you blindly believe what I am saying too? Question it! Test it out for yourself and see what happens.

I frequently talk about the importance of questioning your belief systems. Our belief systems are often put in place for us by others. Some might be true, some might be pure rubbish. So, one must question everything and destroy the belief systems that do not work for you.

Finally, Phiroze's 'push for pull' idea encourages you to experiment. Do the opposite of what the door says but do so gently, just in case you end up damaging the door or the floor or someone's nose on the other side. Gently, test it out before you commit. Remember, this is not rebelling without a cause, this is just experimenting.

So many learnings from a simple door.

In fact, I always wanted to have a door that would only open one way, then put the exact opposite instructions on the inside. Just to see for how long would someone be stuck at the door. It would be a great tool for a job interview. HR, are you listening?

As your habit coach, I want you to have a mind that is free-thinking, curious and questioning. Constantly looking for a better way, or something new. Your super simple habit to start doing just that starts by pushing the 'pull' doors and pulling the 'push' doors. Every time you see a door that says push, first gently pull at it, see if it works this way, and if not, by all means, push it.

Let's bring back the symbolism to doors. Let's make doors stand for curiosity and experimentation and, of course, new beginnings.

Exercise

Let's play a game. All you need for it is a little spontaneity and a couple of curious friends. For the next three days, each of you has to follow the day's instructions given below. And then share your experiences with each other.

Day 1: Do things differently—Take a mundane task that you do daily and find a way to do it differently. It could be as basic as taking a new route while driving to work or making your morning tea/coffee differently. Observe how a seemingly dull task becomes interesting as you add an element of newness to it.

Day 2: Challenge the herd mentality—At home or work, look out for an opportunity where you can 'push' the 'pull' door. Gently question why things are done in a certain way. Explore the possibility of challenging the herd mentality. For example, if it's always the same person doing the chores at home or specific tasks in the office, have a casual conversation and see if you can introduce a small change.

Day 3: Challenge your belief systems— Examine the belief system you live by. Look closely at things you believe to be entirely true. Question them. Think or do the exact opposite of something you've taken for granted and see what happens. Notice if your belief system shakes, changes or stays the same.

At the end of three days, have fun discussing your experiences, the expected and unexpected outcomes, and your learnings too. Make this a daily habit of questioning things in the world around you. It will help you think differently.

The Rich Mindset

In the name of Goddess Laxmi, the revered deity of wealth and prosperity, lies the secret to becoming rich. Her name comes from the Sanskrit word 'lak', which means to perceive and observe. 'Laksh', meanwhile, means goal or objective

I wrote this chapter on Dhanteras, the day we do a small puja for Laxmi, welcoming the goddess into our house. Her entry, we hope, will usher in prosperity—and by prosperity, we mostly mean money.

It is interesting that we often have quite a funny relationship with money. On one hand, we want it and on another, we act as if we don't. 'Oh, money is not important,' we might say, or, 'I am not doing it for the money.' We don't want to appear materialistic and so we create all these excuses and send mixed signals.

Then, there is the way we talk about people who have money. 'Oh, she must be loaded. Everything is easy for her', 'If I had that much money, my life would be so much better', 'He can afford to do that, he has pots of money.' Statements like these are often tinged with jealousy and our own greed.

It seems we have a complicated relationship with money. We want more of it, but don't want to appear as if we are running behind it. However, we can acknowledge that money makes life easier.

In one of the mythological stories, the goddess Laxmi abandons the gods when she feels they have seized wealth with greed and arrogance. The message is clear: looking at things with greed and jealousy is not the way to get rich.

We live in a world where no one ever feels they have enough money. I know so many millionaires who feel they are broke, who feel they have nothing. This is because they are constantly comparing themselves to someone else, someone with more money.

Look around. The media and society today are constantly telling us to get rich. 'Make twenty times your income in one year.' 'Become a millionaire by the age of thirty', and so on. We see fancy cars and big homes and covet them immediately. We are shown a glossy image of success and we start to believe that is what success looks like. But is it really?

The key thing to remember is that there is a big difference between being rich and feeling rich. A billionaire can feel like a poor person, while someone else can have a rich mindset and be at peace with what they have. Am I saying that you should not try to earn more money? No, not at all. The point is to fall in love with what money represents for you, and not with money itself.

Let me say that again, slowly, because this is an important point that I want to emphasise. Fall in love with what money *represents*, do not fall in love with money.

Do you want more money so you can go on holidays? What is stopping you now? Do you want more money to buy a fancy car? Why? What does that car represent for you? Is it a sense of freedom and escape you are seeking? Or, does it represent a rise in status?

I want more money so that I can keep creating things like my podcast, YouTube videos and the habit coaching app and share them for free as gifts. Money for me represents giving back to society, of having the ability to change society.

This is where the first meaning of Laxmi comes in—Lak or perception. Observe and perceive the role of money in your life. What do you want it for? Is it to show off? Is it to give your children a better education? What is the role of money in your life?

This is one of the biggest questions people with a rich mindset ask themselves. By asking this question, you are making your motives clearer to yourself. You will see the greed disappear and the jealousy fall away as you focus on your true intentions.

The next hint, hidden in Goddess Laxmi's name, is 'lakshya' or goal.

The rich mindset is about having a very definite goal in mind for your wealth, your riches. It is not about mindlessly accumulating. It is about working towards an end result, having something you are reaching for.

People with goals succeed because they know exactly what they are going after, right down to how that goal is going to make them feel.

Recently, I have been getting a lot of direct messages on Instagram about financial habits. Most people lament the fact that they are broke. They have a poor mindset towards money and hence constantly feel like they do not have enough money. A poor mindset is one which believes money is bad, yet constantly feels a lack of it. Instead, imagine if they could flip their thinking. They could start thinking with a rich mindset: First, welcoming money into their life by way of opportunities. Second, understanding that money is a tool and they should love and yearn for what that money represents. Third, have a clear goal for what they want to achieve in their lives. It could be a financial goal or something small that is personally fulfilling. Clarity is important.

So, your simple habit that can turn things around for you is a change in your money mindset. It starts by understanding that being rich has nothing to do with what is in your bank account. It is about how you feel about what you have and why you have these things in your life. What is the purpose of your money and what money means to you.

As your habit coach, I want to see all of you feeling financially free, rich and happy!

Exercise

There are three steps to this exercise.

First, let's welcome money into your life. Write a brief note on welcoming money. If Goddess Laxmi represents prosperity to you, then you can address and write a small letter welcoming her into your life with open arms.

Next, imagine you have unlimited wealth at your disposal. Write three things about what that would mean to you. Think of money as a tool here. What are the three things you love and yearn for, the things that more money can make possible to possess or accomplish?

Lastly, set a goal related to what you wrote in the previous step. It can be a financial goal or something else. Bring in clarity as to why you want the money, how much you want it, and how you plan to earn it.

_____

_____

_____

_____

Revisit this goal daily and make a plan to achieve it step by step. Remember to operate from a place of clarity towards wealth creation and not greed or mindless accumulation.

Get Yourself a Shark

I heard an interesting story the other day. Dr Vignesh Devraj, a guest on my podcast, told me a fascinating tale about the Japanese and their taste for fish. Apparently, the Japanese add a small shark to their fish tanks.

Confused? Let me explain.

Back in the day when the Japanese population was small, they would fish just off the coastline. But, as the population grew and their demand for fish increased, they had to start fishing further and further away. This also meant a trip back, with the fish that had been caught kept on ice. The problem with this was that the discerning Japanese could taste the difference. The catch wasn't fresh enough.

To counter this problem, fishing boats came to be made with tanks to hold seawater. This allowed the fishermen to keep the fish alive all the way back to the mainland. You'd think this would have solved the problem. But no, it didn't.

The fish would thrash around and then finally settle down and stop swimming. Apparently this caused the quality of their meat to change. The Japanese could taste this change and did not approve of it.

What more could be done? There was no way to keep the fish swimming in the tank. Finally, some genius decided to put a small shark into the tank with the fish. Sure, the shark would eat some of them, but the others would have a reason to keep swimming. They would have to escape the shark to save their lives!

When we think of our lives and the qualities we want to have, we often only think of positive traits and miss out on negative virtues. Stoic philosophers talked about the positive virtues that we should embody and the negative virtues that we must drop in order to improve our lives.

An example of a negative virtue is complacency. The feeling of satisfaction with our achievements prevents us from observing the dangers that exist around us. We often experience complacency when we are young and being taken care of by our parents. We may experience it in our later lives, too, when we have a stable job, decent income, reasonable comforts and so on—when life seems to be going by smoothly.

I used to be the perfect example of complacency while growing up. I had my family business to join, there was a path that was all laid out for me. There was no need for me to push more than I needed to.

I would waste my days filled with a false sense of satisfaction with myself.

Usually, people are shaken out of their complacency when a big change comes about in their lives. For some it may happen when they get married or when their first child is born—suddenly, they find themselves responsible for another person. For others, it may be when they lose a loved one and have to rethink their lives.

Unless something jolts us out of it, we spend much of our lives in this zone of complacency. We let life pass us by, unaware of the changes taking place around us and, sometimes, within us. For, just like the fish in the Japanese fishing boats, we too start to atrophy or become weak because we do not have any challenge to keep us honest, engaged and active!

As your habit coach, I want to show you that being satisfied is good, but being complacent is not. Just like the Japanese and their fish tanks, we need to add a shark in our lives to wake us up and keep us active.

The state of complacency gives rise to mental and physical health issues. Not moving enough, not eating healthy or sleeping enough can be symptoms. The malaise is complacency. We all need that shark in different aspects of our lives, to drive the complacency away.

The way I did this with my podcast was by making a commitment that each episode will be published on time. Three episodes a week felt impossible in the beginning. The shark in my tank was the audience, the producers, the studio. I had to grow and become stronger to continue churning out three episodes. I had to be consistent. As of writing this book, we are up to five episodes each week. If I had been complacent, I know I would not have gone past episode fifty.

Your super simple habit to move away from living a life of complacency starts by adding a shark to your tank. The shark can be an accountability partner, someone you trust to check in on you and make sure you are doing what you said you would. It can be small penalties related to deadlines or tasks that need to be completed. It can be a financial hit—for instance, pledging to donate Rs 1,000 for every cigarette smoked. Or, it can be the people who depend on you, like your children or employees in your business.

Exercise

Identify one area where you are most comfortable, and where you have a set routine that you enjoy. It can be an area of your career, it can be something in your workout schedule, family time, or weekend routine. Write it down.

Now think about it critically. Does your comfort qualify as complacency? Have you stopped pushing yourself or stopped trying new things?

If yes, think and write down any two actions that can nudge you a little further from your comfort zone.

Create a plan to do these actions.

_____

_____

_____

_____

_____

Have an accountability partner and set a penalty for yourself. This is the key that ensures that you keep to the plan.

Move to different areas of your life where you can do the same exercise.

Reverse Paranoia

Have you heard of Paranoid Personality Disorder (PPD)? It is a mental health condition where the afflicted person is distrustful of everything without reason. They feel that everyone is plotting against them.

It starts off quite simply. You feel you can't trust someone. Then, the number of people you can't trust keeps growing. You start to feel they are all plotting against you and that you are caught in a web of deceit. You can't trust anyone. You feel alone and trapped.

There is no evidence that anyone is out to get you. Yet, these scenarios keep playing in your head. This can become a serious mental condition. It is also hard for the loved ones in your life as they cannot help you, since you do not trust them.

While PPD is a medical condition, many of us have paranoid thoughts. It may not be as extreme, but there is some paranoia that floats inside all our heads. You see people whispering and you feel they are talking about you. You think that your friends are excluding you from things on purpose. People are trying to upset you and anger you or they are trying to sabotage your job or business or friendships. This used to happen to me all the time when I saw people talking when I entered a party or when we were discussing business deals in a meeting.

If we are being honest, we often know that these thoughts have no bearing in reality. And yet, we often cling to our suspicions and unfounded paranoia. Living with these thoughts creates a negative frame of mind. It makes for a negative life! We distance ourselves and feel alone. We do not accept things that happen for our good, instead, we look at them with suspicion. This is because as humans we are wired to be 'loss averse' which means we are constantly trying to protect ourselves from some loss, perceived or not.

We need to create space for vibrant, amazing things to happen in our lives. If we fill up that space with suspicion and negativity instead, we will never be able to welcome that which makes us happy. How can we climb up and help ourselves?

Today, I want to share a habit that is radical, one that is annoyingly happy. I am talking about something I learnt recently called 'reverse paranoia'. It has changed my life.

J.D. Salinger said, 'I'm a kind of paranoiac in reverse. I suspect people of plotting to make me happy.' It's a fantastically radical perspective change. Imagine, if you could see people as always trying to help you or make you happy! The genius of this new perspective is that you spot opportunities far more easily now. This is so because you believe they exist. You're still making assumptions, you're just choosing to make positive ones.

From loss aversion to opportunity magnet! It's not that you suddenly attract opportunities. Rather, you pick up on opportunities you would have previously glossed over because you didn't trust where they were coming from. It truly is life-altering, and as your habit coach, I want you to experience this as well.

So, your super simple habit starts by changing your inner dialogue. It will be forced at first, but within a few days, it will become second nature to you. Start looking at everyone you meet as if they are there to help you on your journey. Look at every single person you see on the road as someone who is going to help you.

It will be weird in the beginning, but soon you will see how this reverse paranoia makes you feel connected to the world around you. You will never feel alone and it will attune your senses to see the best in people. Will there be pitfalls and bad moments? Of course. That is life! But your outlook towards the world will change, and you'll find yourself living that vibrant and amazing life you always wanted.

Exercise

For the next couple of days, observe your thoughts when you meet people—friends, strangers, colleagues or family.

What is the general feeling you get when you meet them? Note them down below.

_____

_____

_____

After that, intentionally start thinking that the person you met, came to help you in some way. Mould your mind to think that they are either bringing you help or an opportunity.

At the end of each day, write down who you met and what were your new thoughts about them.

_____

_____

_____

Keep practising this daily. Soon you will start seeing opportunities flowing your way. This reverse paranoia will make you feel connected to everyone and you will have a fresh positive outlook towards the world!

_____

Stop Catastrophising

The English word 'catastrophe' has its roots in the Greek word 'katastrephein'. 'Kata' means down and 'strephein' means turn. So, the literal meaning of the word 'katastrephein' is 'down turn' or 'turn around'. Isn't it interesting that the word 'catastrophe', in its original form, does not mean disaster? It simply refers to a sudden change.

Now, because most Greek plays were tragedies, the katastrephein were usually sad and dramatic. For instance, a sudden misfortune would kill a family or a violent act would maim the hero.

When the word was included in English, it just meant 'a sudden turn of events at the end of a story'. Hence, it could have been a positive twist as well. For example, the prince finding Cinderella, using the shoe at the end of the story, is also a catastrophe, only a positive one.

However, over time, 'catastrophe' has come to be associated only with negative happenings. Lovers dying, a mother losing her son, a virtuous woman betrayed, the newly married man dying in battle and so on. As part of a play or a movie, it's pure entertainment. It makes us feel for a fleeting moment that our lives are not so bad!

We enjoy that bittersweet ending. It adds an element of drama and makes for an interesting story. Something good happens and then something bad happens.

Have you ever noticed that when everything is going perfectly in the hero's life in a movie, we sometimes prophesise doom? *Something bad is going to happen,* we think to ourselves. The hero has just asked his love to marry him and now he is driving home, music playing, a smile on his face. In our head, we expect a car to come out of nowhere and hit him any second!

This is because we have been programmed to believe that all things will eventually take a turn for the worse, especially if they are running smoothly in the present. We have a tendency to take what we learn from movies and stories and apply it to real life. In doing so, we also begin to expect the worst in our personal lives. We actively start looking for all the things that can go wrong. We assume doom is inevitable, even if everything is going smoothly in our life at present. It's too good to be true, we think. We wait for the plot twist, for tragedy to strike.

What we need to realise is that we are not living in a movie or a Greek tragedy. What happens in the movies is for drama and entertainment. Our lives are not governed by the need for drama. We do not need a plot twist to keep life interesting.

However, our mind keeps going there and looking for all that can go wrong. What if the car breaks down? What if I fall sick? What if my mother disapproves of this marriage?

We immediately jump to the worst possible outcome that is truly Bollywood-worthy. We then obsess over this negative outcome and it begins to take over our lives. The truth is that none of those negative scenarios may actually play out. Still, we live in anticipation of the worst. We ruin our lives with the thought that a catastrophe (in a negative sense!) is about to strike. Worse, we begin to ruin the lives of everyone around us as well by worrying and behaving like everything is going to turn into a disaster.

I call this catastrophising. This is when we make things far worse than they really are by imagining that things will be far worse than they really are.

The best way to deal with catastrophising is to ask yourself: Is there any truth to this? What is a positive catastrophe that might emerge instead of a negative one? If you are going to think up a twist, why not a positive one? This will take a little bit of practice. You must try and make it a habit, especially if you are someone who has a lot of negative thoughts and pictures only the worst possible outcomes.

When you stop thinking of negative outcomes and instead think of positive twists taking you by surprise, you make a change in your brain. Your brain is now geared to be on the lookout for new information that is positive in nature and you start noticing positive things that happen to you.

There is a reason movies and Greek tragedies last only a few hours. Any longer and we would not be able to handle them. Don't turn your life into a sad movie or a Greek tragedy. Thinking up positive plot twists is way more fun than catastrophising.

Exercise

The next time you catch yourself having negative thoughts, observe and write down what you are thinking about. Note your fears and the worst-case scenario that can happen.

Next, ask yourself the following questions and write down the answers.

Is there any truth to your negative thoughts?

Are your fears rational?

Now, think of a positive twist for the same situation. Could this turn of events make your life awesome? Write it down below.

The Importance of Masti

Sometimes, in the humdrum of everyday life, we forget the importance of play. There is a form of play that, in Hindi, is called 'masti'. There is no English word that can accurately describe what it stands for. It is a cross between play and mischief, fun purely for the sake of fun. This is my favourite kind of play. I wish we could live in a state of perennial masti. But as grown-ups, we somehow neglect to have masti in our lives.

Animals, meanwhile, take their playtime quite seriously. Those of us who have more than one pet at home are used to seeing them play or engage in mock fights. They routinely jump, hide, pounce and chase each other around. We believe that they are practising their skills—how to hunt, fight or get away from danger. The other theory is that every time they play, they are strengthening their bond. A bond that will last them a lifetime and will be a source of support.

So, does playing make animals tougher? Does it hone skills they need for their survival? If that is the case, then why do adult animals play as well? Think about dolphins joyfully leaping out of the water and diving back in. Or about whales that have deep diving competitions with each other. What purpose does this act of playing have for these grown-up animals? Even scientists don't have a clear answer for that. It's all still a mystery.

My favourite scientific mystery though, that puzzles scientists to this day, comes all the way from Churchill, Manitoba, on the shores of Hudson Bay in Canada. It is known as the polar bear capital of the world. Two wildlife photographers, who were filming in the area, spotted a polar bear walking towards a chained sled dog. Polar bears have been steadily facing food shortage and this bear clearly looked malnourished. Polar bears are predators and have been known to eat sled dogs.

The photographers started filming the exchange. What happened next was shocking. The polar bear approached the sled dog and started playing with it! The two animals playfully wrestled and bit each other. After a while, the polar bear got up and left. The dog remained unharmed.

Now, what logical sense does it make for an animal to waste its energy playing, especially when it is starving? Clearly, play has an important function in adult lives too.

As kids, we played so many different games. We created—and escaped into—make-believe worlds and, for a while, forgot all our worries. We joked and laughed without a care in the world and danced like no one was watching.

What changed when we became adults? The weight of the world fell on our shoulders and we suddenly became serious.

Everyone's expectations started to weigh us down. We began to lose our sense of individuality and began conforming to the idea of how adults are supposed to behave. Our goals and responsibilities took over our lives. We forgot to take the time to enjoy little moments of our lives daily.

Instead of worlds created by our imagination and playfulness, we now turn to our phones when we want to escape. It takes our attention away from our immediate surroundings but directs it towards distressing news and doomsday WhatsApp forwards. If not that, we passively look at snapshots of other people living it up for social media. We are drained from sitting at home and seeing our life just pass us by.

But who said life has to be this monotonous?

At the end of 2020, I started a support group on Telegram. I put up a link on my Instagram and left it open for anyone to join. I created that group because I realised that people were going through mental and emotional trauma at the time, and I felt it would help to just talk to others.

A hundred or so people joined the group and the first day was a volley of messages back and forth. People were asking each other about their well-being and sharing what they were going through. They were asking me questions about life, love and self-worth.

Remember, we were all strangers in the group. But we opened up and shared parts of our lives with one another. Soon, the nature of the conversation completely changed from serious to playful. People started joking with each other. They began to play games. We even started writing poems for each other.

The whole group began to play. A group that I had created to commiserate and share bad news with was now an island of positivity in a sea of negativity.

The people in the group were desperate to have fun. At that dire time, when the only WhatsApp messages being circulated were desperate cries of help for oxygen cylinders and depressing news of death and the lockdown, this little playful group had become a place to relax and just chill.

The human need for play is strong. In fact, at the worst of times, we need it more. We need the relief that unadulterated masti brings us.

As your habit coach, I want you to add masti back into your life. Find those little moments of playfulness. Crack a joke, tease a friend, play a prank, act foolish and laugh your heart out for no reason at all.

Add masti to the chores you do every day. Mundane tasks can be made fun!

Don't feel guilty about fun. Remember, masti acts as a break from the stress of the day, from the bad news we receive and from the seriousness of our lives.

Adopt this simple habit by consciously taking a break from the seriousness of life. Then add masti to things you do every day. Add masti to dinner table conversations. Add masti to your daily chores and even to work. Think about how something can be made fun. Make masti a habit and it will become a part of your life forever.

Remember, being an adult does not mean we cannot play or have fun!

Exercise

Think of a time in your life when you didn't have the responsibilities that weigh you down today. Go back to that time and remind yourself what it was that brought you joy. Was it spending time with friends, joking and laughing? Was it dancing your heart out? Was it playing pranks on each other?

Write down a few things that you enjoyed before adult life took over.

_____

_____

_____

_____

Next, promise yourself three actions in the coming week that you will do which will bring the same amount of joy and fun back into your life. This doesn't have to be something that will take much time away from your busy day. It can be the smallest act.

_____

_____

_____

_____

Repeat the previous exercise every week for the first few weeks until this becomes not just a habit but part of who you are, and your personality. Add masti to the chores you do every day. Mundane tasks can be made fun!

Are You a Potato or an Egg?

Benjamin Waddy Maughan was a house painter in London. In 1868, he invented the first water heater. He named this terrific invention 'geyser', after the hot springs. Maughan's invention involved heating up the water by putting a burner underneath the cold water pipes. The burners would heat the water as it passed through the pipes. And voila—there would be hot water! His invention inspired the Norwegian engineer Edwin Ruud to make a water heater with a tank that would store the hot water. And the rest, as we say, is history.

Nowadays we just flip a switch and hot water comes out of our taps. It's hard for us to imagine a time when this was not the case and heating water was a tedious and time-consuming affair. While readily available hot water makes our life easier, it is often used as a metaphor for discomfort. You ask someone how they are doing and if they say, 'I am in hot water with this new deal,' what they are basically saying is that the world around them is stressing them out. Or that there is too much pressure on them.

Being in hot water is synonymous with being in an uncomfortable spot. But does it always have to be so? Let's do a little experiment. Put a pot of water to boil. When the water is boiling, slip in an egg and a potato into the water. Let them boil for a while. Sounds like a recipe, doesn't it?

When the water, with the egg and the potato in it, has been boiling for a bit, you'll notice that the egg is harder than it was. The boiling water makes it less likely to shatter. The potato, meanwhile, is softer than it was. You can mash it up now.

Whether one is better than the other is irrelevant. Is being hard good? Is soft somehow bad? One is protein and the other is a carb. Forget all that because that's not what matters to us in this moment.

The essence of the experiment is that both things were exposed to the same stimulus: hot water. The hot water does not make or break you, it just exists. What makes or breaks you is what you are made of. Now, a potato cannot become an egg and an egg cannot become a potato. But luckily, humans are quite versatile. We have the ability to make choices.

You will notice that when you expose two people to the exact same stimulus, they end up making different choices. It is these choices that determine whether we are hard or soft, strong or weak, better or worse.

When you are thrown in hot water, don't get into the habit of complaining about it. Don't start wishing for the water temperature to change. Instead, learn to make choices that improve you. Use the hot water as a stimulus for growth. For example, if you are in a very demanding sales job, your targets and the pressure associated with them may be the hot water. Use that pressure to become better at your job. Learn new sales techniques and interesting pitches to make proposals and close sales.

Sometimes, what we perceive as a difficult time is actually an opportunity to discover our hidden strengths. Almost all the people in the world that we admire, have been in boiling hot water at some point in their lives. Even my life changed after I went through my own soak in boiling water. The environment would not change, so I did.

I have three habits that you can inculcate to make the most of a stressful situation you find yourself in.

The first habit is to stop complaining and comparing yourself to others. When you stop complaining, you begin to take responsibility. And don't compare, because we cannot see the hardships other people are going through. Water is transparent, but we only have visibility over the boiling water in our own pot!

The second habit is to acknowledge your situation and attempt to get stronger to pull yourself out of it. Instead of constantly fighting the pain, you must learn to work with it, to work despite it. Review the plan every day. Take one small step at a time and work your way out.

The third habit to adopt is to keep yourself positive, no matter how hard things get. This may seem tough, but our mental well-being determines much of our abilities. It's important we nurture ourselves.

Every day, write down three things you are grateful for. Listen to podcasts and watch videos that fill you with happiness and positivity. Do one thing to foster positivity every day as a habit.

Remember, what the world throws at you is never in your control. You can only control what you do with it. You can choose to be a potato or an egg. What will you choose?

Exercise

Identify the current situation in your life where you feel like you are in boiling hot water. It could be anything that is stressful or uncomfortable or challenging in your life.

Write down your dominant thoughts about this situation.

Read what you have written and notice if you are complaining or comparing yourself to something or someone. If yes, take ownership of the problem. If you cannot solve the problem right away, take responsibility for how you are going to handle and feel about the situation.

Rethink, rephrase and write down your thoughts again now.

Next, make a plan of how you can become stronger, how you can pull yourself out of the hot water. Revisit this plan every day and take one small step at a time towards it.

_____

_____

_____

Lastly write three things that you are grateful for in your life daily (Use the format below).

This will bring a positive outlook to your thoughts. Fill your mind with positivity and happiness.

I am grateful for _____

_____

_____

_____

You will embrace the pain as part of growth and take it in your stride

You can then choose to be the potato or the egg based on what you decide to do.

It's Not Impossible

Impossible is nothing. Let me explain. Did you know that as little as a few centuries ago it was believed that if humans travelled faster than 80 kilometres per hour, they would die? It was believed that the person would not be able to breathe at that speed, or that their head would explode. We think about that now and laugh, but people were afraid when the first car that ran at that speed was invented.

It is crazy just how many things we believed were impossible, till suddenly one day they became possible. Things like flying, or the humble light bulb. Things we take completely for granted today were once things that were considered unimaginable.

When I was in college, a family friend told me that he'd heard of scientists who were working on a phone where the caller's picture would appear when they called on it. I laughed at him and said that was impossible. At that point, I couldn't imagine a phone with a colour screen, let alone one that showed pictures.

But, in my lifetime itself, we have done things that were thought to be impossible once. The Zoom meetings that we hate and take for granted now were once a technology that used to be seen only in the fanciest of boardrooms. I remember going to these boardrooms and wondering, *Wow, imagine having people from all over the world joining.* Each minute of those calls was over a thousand rupees! It was crazy.

To think that not so long after, I would be setting up meetings and conducting workshops for people sitting in Europe, all from my farm in Karjat. The impossible became possible within a very short time!

I know people who use the word 'impossible' all the time. It is part of their everyday speech. I have multiple issues with that word being used. Firstly, it shuts the door to making something possible. By this, I mean that when we believe something is impossible, we stop trying to do it. We give up even before we begin. The fact is, things aren't as difficult once we take that first step. As I always say, starting is more than half the battle.

Secondly, once we dismiss something as impossible we forget about it and move on to something else. It is forgotten altogether. Lastly, we stop using our imagination. This is the biggest crime. Our imagination is the tool we need to be able to visualise and plan—to be able to see into the future. It is the tool that we use to dream.

Everything that was once believed to be impossible but exists now, started off as a dream. A dream that someone turned into a reality. They saw into the future and believed it was possible. Then, they took the required steps and worked backwards till they made it happen. Being able to visualise the future is the key to making the impossible, possible.

What does this have to do with you and your life? Let's see.

We keep jumping to conclusions: I will never be a professional pastry chef. I will never have a million dollars. I will never own a Ferrari. And the like. We feel these are impossible goals to have. But the truth is, they are impossible only because we don't know how to do these things yet.

'Yet' is the operative word here. Right now, in the present, you can't do it. But imagine that in the future you can. Then, figure out what you need to do to achieve it. Imagination is powerful. Don't shut it down by using the silly word 'impossible.'

So, your super simple habit to have the life of your dreams starts by never using the word 'impossible' ever again. Instead, start referring to your goals as 'future possible.' You will slowly start believing that it is possible for you to achieve anything.

And if nothing else, remember that if Tom Cruise can do it, so can you!

Exercise

Remember an instance from your recent past where you had a vision or a dream that you did not go after because you thought it was impossible. Mention it below.

_____
_____

Now rephrase the same dream by adding the word 'yet' to it and write it down below.

For example, if you wanted to buy an expensive designer watch, instead of saying 'It's impossible,' rephrase it to 'I haven't bought my designer watch yet.'

_____
_____

Now let loose your imagination and write down any three ideas that can help you make your dream come true.

_____
_____
_____
_____
_____
_____
_____
_____
_____

Do this exercise as often as you can. Make 'future possible' part of your vocabulary and remove 'impossible' from your thoughts, vocabulary, and life!

Teflon Mind

Did you know that lizards can climb walls with the help of little hair on their feet? These tiny, fine hair bristles, called setae, enable the lizard to climb almost any surface. They can even walk on ceilings, upside down!

There is, however, one surface that lizards cannot climb—the man-made surface called Teflon. Yes, the same black coating on our frying pans. Teflon is so smooth that there are no gaps for the tiny hair on the feet of lizards to attach themselves to. So now all of you who are scared of those lizards at home know what you have to do. Teflon coating on the walls!

Teflon was not originally created for frying pans. In fact, it has been used in all sorts of places. For example, armour-piercing bullets use Teflon to prevent the barrel of the gun from wearing down. Needles used by doctors are coated with Teflon to make them less painful. Teflon was even used for the Mars mission!

Recently, in an attempt to stop using Teflon cookware, I was frying an egg in a stainless-steel frying pan. Or rather, I was trying to. No matter what I did, I could not make the egg come off the surface. It just kept getting stuck. I would try to gently lift it off the pan, but it wouldn't comply. Pretty soon, it would start burning and cause a mess. I tried egg after egg with the same result. I could not figure out if the pan was too hot or too cold. Was there not enough oil in the pan?

Then I learnt that you have to treat the surface of a regular pan by burning off some oil. It is important to find the right temperature for the surface before one begins cooking. This is achieved by sprinkling some water on it. I did all that and was finally able to cook an egg tolerable enough to eat. However, nothing could beat the way my eggs turned out in a Teflon frying pan.

Our minds are exactly like the stainless-steel frying pan, and our thoughts are like eggs. Sometimes, they stick inside our heads, even if we don't want them to. They start burning and cause a mess. Then they become hard to remove and leave burnt bits everywhere. When we get a thought that doesn't leave us, we sometimes overthink it. That is like turning up the heat. It does nothing but make the thought burn.

Sometimes we try to distract ourselves with other things. The thought is still there in our minds. It is still stuck and will eventually start burning if we leave it there unattended, quite like an egg in an unattended frying pan.

Instead, we can try treating our mind with other things. Gratitude practices and journalling are great places to start. These practices help condition us to not get attached to our thoughts. In other words, they help us 'treat' our mind.

As your habit coach, I don't want you to just have a well-seasoned mind. I want you to experience a Teflon mind—a mind where thoughts come and then slip off; where there is no attachment to the thought.

This state of detachment comes when we practice meditation. We think of meditation as a state of emptiness, a state of no thoughts. This is not correct. Meditation is a state where thoughts come and go freely in our minds without us overthinking or getting too attached to them. They simply come and go. No agonising, no worrying, and no burning them either.

Practising meditation allows us to get a Teflon mind. I want you to become curious about meditation, about the concept and the process, so that you can start to do the self-work needed to get a Teflon mind.

The first step towards building this habit is nurturing a curious and inquisitive mind. Find out more about meditation. See what its benefits are. Then, begin incorporating meditation into your day. Set a fixed time for your own meditation practice. For example, I meditate every day at 6:30 a.m. sharp. Some of you might have learnt meditation and have now stopped meditating. Get back to your routine and make meditation a practice for life. Make it a habit first.

If you have never meditated, start by sitting still and observing your thoughts. Notice the ones that stick. See how you can allow them to just slide off. Imagine yourself smoothly sliding an egg or flipping a pancake off a Teflon pan. Through meditation every one can achieve a Teflon mind.

Exercise

List three practices that can help you manage your mindset. These can be journalling or regular gratitude practice or anything else that helps you to feel centered before you start the day.

Set aside a time in your morning routine for at least one of these.

Now, add meditation to this list and plan your new morning routine. Write it down below.

If you have done meditation before, resume the practice even if it is for 10 minutes in a day.

If you are new to meditation, do not force yourself to stop having thoughts when you meditate. Observe your thoughts and slowly learn to meditate. Imagine your thoughts sliding off, like the egg on a Teflon pan.

Practise this daily for a month, and you will realise, that 'you' are not your thoughts and they are just transient visitors in your Teflon mind!

Are You Comfortable?

Did you know that Mallakhamb originated in India, way back around 200 BCE? While today it is viewed as a form of gymnastics, performed by wrestlers, it was actually a form of martial arts that was practised by wrestlers and warriors of the time to improve their strength and flexibility.

Mallakhamb has many forms. It can be performed on a rope hanging from the ceiling, or on a large log of wood that forms a solid pole, 8.5 feet high. There are many other variations of Mallakhamb as well. Wrestlers used the Mallakhamb techniques to enhance their grip. Recently, Mallakhamb has been added as an act to the world-famous Cirque du Soleil. It is performed by our very own Indian Mallakhamb masters.

We even have a Mallakhamb world championship now. The last championship took place in Budapest and the next is in America. I was surprised at how mainstream this ancient martial art form is slowly becoming.

Recently, when I walked into my gym, all pumped to do a hardcore leg workout, the guys at the reception asked me to try the Mallakhamb class. I had attended my first Mallakhamb class about four years ago. I faintly remembered enjoying it and so decided to give it another go.

The class was going great. We had two instructors: a woman who had been practising for nine years and a man who had been doing it for eleven. Everything they did looked easy and effortless. It was all smooth till I went on the pole. It was difficult!

I particularly struggled with a pose where I had to stand facing the pole, then bend all the way forward, touch my head to the floor and grip the pole with my hands from the back. Yeah ... with my flexibility, that was not happening.

Another student tried the same pose. She could manage to get into that position. Then the teacher said something that blew my mind ... He asked her, 'Are you comfortable?' Comfortable? How on earth could that position be comfortable for anyone? That was easily the most unnatural, uncomfortable position known to humankind. But then he said something more. He said, 'For all of us this was difficult in the beginning. But now it is normal.'

And that is the key.

When we start something new, it is often uncomfortable. Every new habit is difficult to build. You wonder how other people manage. Take something as simple as waking up early. For so many of us, it is easy-peasy. Yet for others, to drag oneself out of bed at an early hour is uncomfortable—nay, impossible. Same is the case with exercise or intermittent fasting. We look and wonder how others do it so easily.

As your habit coach, I want to let you in on a secret—it starts difficult for everybody. No one has it easy or comfortable when they get started. But they persist and over a period of time, after being consistent, the 'difficult' habit becomes almost natural and the person becomes comfortable practising it.

I want you to realise that when you are uncomfortable, that means you are on the right track. You have to push past that stage and reach a place of ease. This applies to all new habits you want to make a part of your life. Persist and wait for the magic to happen.

Exercise

Write down a habit that you tried for a while, found difficult and stopped mid-way.

_____

Challenge yourself to follow it for the next thirty days. Write down your mission statement for this habit formation.

_____
_____
_____
_____
_____

Use a habit tracker, put a big tick or happy smiley face on days you keep the habit.

Have a plan B for days when you find it difficult to practise the habit.

For example, if your habit is to go to the gym and lift weights, on the days when you find it difficult, define a smaller set of exercises to do.

_____
_____
_____

Whenever you feel uncomfortable following the habit, come back to this exercise, and read your mission statement and your plan B. Soon, you will cross the bridge and move to the other side where the habit would've become a part of you.

Busyness

Have you heard of the Northumbrian word 'bisignes'? It means to be careful, anxious or busy. In fact, it is from here that the word 'business' originates—the state of being busy or occupied with things.

This idea of constantly being in a state of busyness is what people believe running a business is all about. Rushing here, rushing there and dealing with 35,000 things. You have no time for anything. You constantly feel like you need to play catch up with to-do lists and so on. And it's not specific to just business; we feel like that in our jobs as well.

However, that's not what I want to talk about here.

Instead, I want to talk about the 'busyness' mindset. This is the mindset where people feel that they need to always be doing something. The feeling of being busy makes them feel that they are doing something worthwhile. Their self-worth is linked to how busy they are. Many clients of mine subscribe to this mindset. The way I see it, it has three big issues.

The first is that people plagued by this busyness mindset cannot relax. They are always running around after things and have no sense of calm. Being around them feels like being trapped in a whirlwind. Your peace is threatened. More importantly, their own inner peace is disturbed and hence they find it very difficult to calm down.

The second big concern with the busyness mindset is that people who have it, actively look for problems to solve. They need something to be a disaster or a distraction around them, in order to be busy. Ask yourself: Does this sound like me? If it does, then I want you to become even more aware of what happens next, which is self-sabotage.

At this stage, you purposely do things that can be disastrous and can cause issues in the future. You leave things half done so that you have something to keep you busy. Or you may take on too much so that you can get a sense of busyness.

The final issue with having a busyness mindset is that it eventually starts affecting your health. Your sleep cycle gets affected. You open yourself up to all sorts of lifestyle-related illnesses. And all this leads to a dip in your immunity.

In order to stop being busy all the time, the first thing I want you to do is to find out if you have a busyness mindset. Is it something you are constantly occupied with? Knowing and accepting something is always the first step to making a change.

The next thing to do is to rid yourself of all the time-consuming, unproductive things in your life. Things that keep you busy but do not add to the quality of your life in any way need to go. You will have to be absolutely ruthless about cutting these things out of your life. They have all at some point made you feel important and busy, and will seem essential. But remember, you have to do it.

Busy activities are like quicksand, they can just suck you in and gobble you up. Do not step into the quicksand! Keep busyness away and focus instead on activities that lead to real productivity.

Your super simple habit starts by realising what the things that keep you busy are. The next step is to start getting rid of these activities. Don't attach your self-worth to them. Instead, get into the habit of asking yourself: Is this productive busyness or unproductive busyness? You will notice that most of it will be unproductive.

Bring a sense of freedom and calm back to your life.

Exercise

Write down five things in your routine that take up most of your time.

Now analyse which of these are not contributing to your well-being, quality of life, or income. Strike these out from your list. Write a new list below.

Next, write down five activities (big or small) in your day that keep you busy.

Ask yourself if each of these contributes to productive 'busyness' or unproductive 'busyness'.

Strike those which contribute to unproductive 'busyness'. Write the new list below.

_____

_____

_____

_____

Make sure you do not do anything that is not on these lists. Be mindful of where you spend your time.

Regain control of your time and freedom in your life!

_____

Be the First or Be the Last

The oldest recorded stampede took place in the year 66. Not 1966, but 66 CE. It happened when a Roman soldier decided to provoke Jewish pilgrims, on their way to the temple on the day of Passover, by showing his bottom and shouting profanities. His vulgar words angered the Jewish youth, some of whom picked up stones and flung them at him.

The Romans called for reinforcements and this led to panic among the Jews, who began to run helter-skelter. This caused a stampede where ten thousand Jews lost their lives. They were trampled to death. It's unreal to imagine that the deadliest stampede in history took place because of one mooning soldier.

There is another disheartening statistic. India has the highest number of notable stampedes in the world—twenty-six. It is partly because of our large population for sure, but there is something else as well—herd mentality.

Stampedes are very common among herd animals. When one of them runs, they all start running together. You will never hear of a stampede among lions or tigers. This is because, though they may hunt in packs, they do not follow the herd system.

The herd system is based on the principle of safety in numbers. The more animals in the herd, the safer they are. This is because there are more eyes to see, more ears to listen to a prey approaching and more noses to smell incoming danger. Apart from that, if you are in the middle of the herd, you are safe, as the chances of a tiger reaching you in case of an attack are minuscule.

Somewhere along the line, humans also began to think of themselves as herd animals. We began to feel safe in numbers. We did whatever everyone else was doing, with the mistaken belief that it would keep us secure.

However, there is a big difference between social animals and herd animals. Humans are social animals. We need to interact with people. We're not all the same. We need others to help us in the areas where we may be lacking and, in turn, we support them in areas where they need our assistance. Social animals understand original thinking; it's a big part of our interactions and helps in problem-solving. We are not herd creatures.

The problem with following the herd is that there is no room to think differently. We have no control over our destiny. In fact, we relegate our choices to others—whatever they do, we do. We blindly follow. After all, that is the rule of the herd.

If you want proof of this behaviour, just search online for a herd of sheep falling off a cliff. It's surprisingly common. In one video, the shepherd watches in horror as one sheep jumps off a cliff and the others just follow suit.

It is very sad and it points to the horror that herd mentality can bring about. Sometimes, we don't realise that we get stuck in this mentality too, and do things without thinking.

Want proof? Think of how we queue up to board an airplane. We rush to stand in line when we all know that the flight is not going anywhere without us. We know there is an order in which the boarding takes place and yet we can't help ourselves.

I used to travel a lot when I had just begun working at my company. I took close to four flights a week. That's when I had my first realisation about how peculiarly the passengers were behaving, and with no justifiable reason except to follow the herd. I formed a habit that I want to share with you.

I decided that I would either be the first or the last in a situation, but never would I be in the middle. That could mean being the first in line or being the last person to board. The first in a competition or the last in a competition ... you get the drift.

For example, I am the first habit coach. When I started, there was no such thing as a habit coach. I created the category. Being first at something gives you the power to make decisions. You have the power to choose and be a leader.

You wouldn't imagine it, but being the last at something gives you certain advantages too. It is an opportunity to learn from everyone else's mistakes. For example, I once went on a trek where we had to cross a river. I decided to go last so I could observe where everyone was placing their feet. By the end of it, I had a pretty good idea of which stone would topple over and which one was too slippery.

Being first is being original. You get to make the rules. Being last, when a conscious decision, is great, for you learn from the mistakes of others. It's being in the middle—being just a part of the herd—that's uninspiring. Why give up your power when you can do so much more?

So, your simple habit starts by stepping out of your herd mentality. If everyone seems to be doing something, stop and question it. Choose to go first or go last when a situation presents itself. No one remembers the person in the middle. Mostly, that person only follows the ones before him; he does nothing remarkable. If you want an awesome life, you have to break away from the herd.

Nothing good comes from being stuck in the middle.

Exercise

The objective of this exercise is to train your mind to break away from the herd mentality.

So when you have something new to try out, an idea, or an exploratory project, write down your answers to these questions.

Is it something that's unique and special to you, your talents? How so?

_____
_____
_____

Do you believe in it wholeheartedly? Why or why not?

_____
_____
_____

Are you ok to meet a few failures along the way to success?

_____
_____
_____

The idea behind these questions is to probe your thinking. It is to train your mind to move away from being safe. Being safe is the easiest option and that's why it doesn't come with any merit.

Next, whenever you have a group activity, ask these questions and choose your position strategically.

Do you want to be the first to do it and take the risk and reward?

_____
_____
_____

or

Do you want to watch others, learn, plan your move and then proceed?

_____
_____
_____

_____

Notice, I never mentioned the middle. It's because, from now on, in any activity or any endeavour, you have to choose first or last, based on what is right for you at that time. You have to move away from being safe. Being in the middle is being a nobody. So leave that for the herd and march ahead!

_____

Copycat

Who would've thought that arthritis would lead to the invention of the photocopying machine? Confused? Let me tell you about it. Chester Carlson was a physicist, an inventor and a patent attorney. He invented xerography, the science of photocopying, in 1938. At the time, he was suffering from a bad case of arthritis.

Arthritis made it difficult for Carlson to rewrite everything by hand. He wanted to find a solution for making a large number of copies easily. In 1942, he obtained a patent for his invention, which he initially called electrophotography.

We, of course, know the process by the name of Xerox, which was actually the company that developed and sold these photocopiers. Their first model was huge and occupied half a room. That wasn't all—if you printed too many copies on it, one after another, it would catch fire. So, guess what? The first Xerox machines were sold with an accompanying fire extinguisher!

Ever since the photocopier was invented, people have been using it to scan their body parts for fun—hands, face, butts and so on. In fact, 20 per cent of all repairs for photocopiers come from people breaking the glass by sitting on it to scan their bottoms. It is a trend!

That brings me to what I really want to talk about. Over the past few years, I have been noticing a strange thing that is taking place all over. As soon as something starts 'trending' we immediately try and copy it, following the trend somewhat mindlessly.

This is not an entirely new phenomenon, of course. Before the internet and social media took over our lives, trends were about the clothes we wore. Bell bottoms were the trend when my parents were in college and then again when I was. So were bright flashy clothes. Right now, it's those high-waisted pants and baggy jeans. Notice how everyone appears to look the same!

When we follow a trend, we are basically copying what someone else has already done. We are blindly following something that someone else has discovered or created. It is someone else's original thought that we are piggybacking on.

On social media today, there are two big ways in which this idea of copying exists. The first is copying people's knowledge almost word for word and sharing it as your own. It is so easy to repackage something original and claim it as your own. An idea that probably took someone else months of their life to research and understand is copied in three minutes.

Let's put aside the ethics behind doing something like that, since ethics are personal.

I want to focus on the injustice we do ourselves by copying. I remember, as a student, I would take all the notes from my friend, Farsheed, in school and get them photocopied. He would work hard by writing things down in class. He would go home and make notes from the textbooks and I would just blindly photocopy them. In college, it was my friend Poorna I copied from and during my MBA, it was Kamlesh. They did the hard work and I did the copying. As a result, they were always in the top ten of the class and I was in the bottom ten.

You see, in the process of making original notes they had understood the material while I was just copying. As a result, I never became a good student. I never improved in any of the things I copied. After all, it is the effort you put in that eventually pays you back.

So many people are now giving free advice online—on nutrition, exercise, finances or business—not having studied those things themselves, or even having read a single research study about the subject. Not only is this dangerous for people consuming the information, it is harmful for the person who has just copied the information from somewhere and is repeating it.

Similarly, I find the way reels are trending on Instagram a bit disturbing. One person makes something brand new with their own voice, their choice of music, their choreography or activity. Then we just blindly copy it. Of course, we might add our own little twist to it, but you have not created something that is uniquely you.

When we thoughtlessly follow trends, we are shutting down our own creative expression. We are following the herd and losing our ability to be creative. You will notice that the people who are doing well online are the ones making their own fresh content. Reels, the way they are today, are just teaching us to copy others.

So, your simple habit starts by understanding the difference between inspiration and copying. Inspiration is when you see something original and use an aspect of it to create something new and amazing for yourself. Copying is when you take 90 per cent of something and tweak it.

Form the habit of asking yourself, with anything you do: Is this copying or is this being inspired?

As your habit coach, I want you to realise that the world belongs to the dreamers, original thinkers and creators. See how you can do the hard work to actually become creative instead of being a copy. Do something brand new.

Exercise

The next time you have an idea before you implement it, ask yourself these questions:

Is your idea totally original?

_____
_____
_____

If not, is it truly inspired or merely copied?

_____
_____
_____

Are you doing this to follow a trend?

_____
_____
_____

If your idea seems to follow what the herd is thinking, ask yourself, which one aspect of it do you like the most?

_____
_____
_____

How can you take that aspect, work hard, put your creative spin on it and make it entirely yours?

_____
_____
_____

Do this exercise every time you have an idea and soon your creativity will take over. You will realise originality never goes out of style!

What If

We are quite used to eating and walking here in India or in America. Take-away fast food, in fact, is a whole sub-culture in itself. It is a sign of our busy lives that we think about food as something we just need to get done with. A quick roll or sandwich on our way to a meeting and we're done.

However, when I went to Japan, I noticed that if you bought your food from a street food vendor, you would have to stand nearby, finish it and only then would you move on. In Japan, it is considered impolite to walk while eating and rarely will you see people doing that. Unless, of course, you are in one of the touristy food streets of Osaka.

It is the same in Italy; to walk while eating is thought to be rude. It is considered disrespectful to the effort that was taken to cook the food. Disrespectful to the ingredients even. Think about it—you cannot be enjoying the meal if you are worried about where you have to be next!

The Italians and the Japanese take great pride in their food. No wonder both countries are known for their unique flavours and cuisines. On that note, I want to share something that happened recently. I was at my friend Sameer Shetty's house for lunch. His wife Aditi and he are super-duper cooks and they love hosting people while trying different recipes.

That night Aditi had made panna cotta for dessert. An Italian dish, its very name means cooked cream. The dish has cream and gelatin cooked to a lovely silken texture. It's one of my favourite desserts and I was looking forward to it.

When she brought the dish out, Aditi revealed that she had made it with coconut milk and then topped it with caramel and ... fish sauce. Yes, you read that correctly. Fish sauce!

When I heard that, I nearly fell off my chair. I could not even imagine what that would be like. Fish sauce is the most pungent tasting and smelling of the sauces used in Southeast Asian cuisine, and here was a delicate panna cotta. How was it ever going to work? Quaking with fear, I put a tiny amount of the caramel sauce on the panna cotta and tasted it.

I kid you not, it was one of the most divine things I had ever tasted. It was simply brilliant!

Now, that is the thing about food and cooking. Everything, at some point in time, must have sounded ridiculous to someone else. It may even have sounded impossible, but only till someone actually did it. The most outlandish idea can transform into something epic, but someone needs to try it out first.

As adults, we have lost our sense of wonder. We evaluate ideas too fast, often before ever trying them out. Imagine if Aditi had seen that recipe of a fish sauce caramel panna cotta, and said 'Nah, that's too funky. Impossible for that to taste good.'

The habit of creativity is all about moments like that. It's about seeing two things that have seemingly no similarities whatsoever and then wondering, 'What if?' Creativity is born out of such 'what-if' moments in life.

The first touchscreen phone possibly came about because someone asked the question, 'What if there was a phone with no buttons?' The idea for Spiderman was most likely born from asking, 'What if a man could do everything a spider can?' All the creative things around you were born out of the fundamental question—what if?

So, your super simple habit to boost your creativity starts by asking the question, 'What if?' Imagine two things that clearly do not go together and ask, what if? What if alligators turned vegetarian? What if cars could talk?

As adults, the world of imagination slowly recedes into the background as we are asked instead to focus on the reality of the world around us. We are told to discard 'what ifs'. If we all heeded that advice, what a boring world that would be. A world where we would never get to experience Aditi's panna cotta with fish sauce and caramel!

Exercise

For this exercise, include a couple of your friends, siblings, or cousins to play along. Let your creative juices flow and make things more interesting!

For the next three days, each of you must come up with one 'what if' idea daily.

At the end of three days, you will have a total of nine such creative ideas to choose from.

You can pick any three of these and try them out during the rest of the week together.

At least one idea from each person has to be tried out by everybody.

And whichever idea is selected must be tried by all three together.

At the end of three days, the whackiest idea, the one that brings the most fun and enjoyment wins the game!

Wisdom and Reflection

Did you know that the earliest mirrors were made of water? The mirror consisted of a bowl that was painted black inside and had water filled in it. The idea was to create the same effect we get when we look at our reflection in a lake or a pond. These mirrors were replaced by black volcanic glass that was polished to form a reflective surface. Later, mirrors were made using copper disks, which were polished until they had a reflective surface. Very often, these are what we find from the Egyptian and Mesopotamian ages.

As soon as any culture had a mirror, it allowed people to look at themselves. It allowed them to dress up or accentuate aspects of themselves, while earlier they would have relied on others to help them.

When we have the ability to see ourselves as someone else sees us, it ignites in us the desire to change and improve ourselves. While I couldn't verify the factual accuracy of its attribution to Aristotle, a quote that I came across on Instagram made me think. It read: 'Wisdom is an equal measure of experience plus reflection.'

Let's break this line down. Wisdom is something that we all want in our lives. We want to be able to make wise choices, give wise advice and live a life of wisdom. However, we do not become wise by sitting in our chairs and watching Netflix or a documentary on the History channel. That is not wisdom. It is just information or knowledge.

We become wise through experience. That means getting out of your chair, out of your home and actually experiencing the world around you. It means trying new things, making new mistakes and opening yourself up to new friends and new acquaintances. It means going on adventures.

These are the things that most of us don't do. We do not spend time doing new things each day. Our lives are fairly routine and set. However, if you get into the habit of trying something new each day, you end up growing with experience.

The next thing that we need to do is reflect. What does this mean? How are we supposed to reflect? Most of us react to the experiences that take place in our lives. If we try something new but face failure, we immediately react and either think we are not good enough or blame the other person. We are trapped in the stimulus and reaction phase. As soon as something happens, we instantly react to it. We don't pause to think.

There is so much anger in the world today. Why are people constantly reacting and becoming so angry with their experiences? If I have a bad experience in a restaurant, I have to immediately tell all forty-five people who follow me on Twitter!

Is that a wise thing to do? Is there wisdom in reacting this way—instantly and intensely?

This is where the second part comes in—reflection. It is the ability to look at oneself and our own thoughts and feelings. It is like holding up a mirror to your mind and seeing what is really going on there.

Now, most of us spend our lives overthinking and obsessing over what has happened or what is going to happen, and this turns into anxiety or sadness. This is because we are looking at our actions or our life with a very biased view.

The key to reflection is to have an unbiased view of your mind. See things as they are, without them being distorted. We have all been to a circus where we have seen these mirrors that make us appear short or tall or fat. Those are distortions.

We need to teach ourselves to reflect without bias and without distortion. We can do this through practice. It takes time to get good at cleaning the mirror of your mind and actually reflecting well.

So, your super simple habit starts by choosing a quiet time each day for your reflections. Ideally, it should be the first thing in the morning or the last thing at night. Sit and just think about an experience you had that day or recently.

Observe that event with complete clarity, without allowing any beliefs or preconceived notions to cloud your judgement. Think about what you learnt from that experience. Think about what you will do differently next time.

In the same way as the invention of the mirror changed the way we approached our physical selves, this habit of reflection can change the way we approach our mental selves.

Exercise

Wisdom is the equal measure of experience and reflection. Let's do two activities for this exercise.

Observe your routines—daily and weekly. How often do you have new experiences that help you become wiser in life?

Now, write down three new experiences that you will add to your life in the coming month.

Remember, with each new experience, you will learn, grow and become wiser.

Next, after doing a new thing each week, reflect on the experience.

Do not judge the experience as good or bad. Stay unbiased and write three observations and learnings from your experience. Train your mind to think and reflect.

You can reflect on the events of your day daily in the morning or evening by sitting in a quiet place.

Develop reflection as a habit, hold the mirror to your mind as often as you can and become the wisest person you can be.

Grow by 10x

Let's talk about the letter 'x'. Did you know that this letter can be traced back to 820 CE Baghdad? Ancient manuscripts, like the *Al-Jabr*, talk about the rules of algebra. All unknown variables were referred to as 'šay' which, translated into English, meant 'things'. For example, an equation would read: 4 things equal to 20.

Later, when the *Al-Jabr* was being translated into Spanish, the word 'šay' was spelt 'Xei'. This, over the course of time, became 'X', which is now widely used to represent the unknown. We have X-ray for unknown rays. And Malcolm X used the letter as his surname to represent all his unknown ancestors!

There are obviously other theories on how 'x' became the torture device for students learning algebra all over the world. Personally, nothing fills me with more dread than trying to find the value of 'x'. Here, though, I want to share a concept made famous by Grant Cardone. His brand is called 10x, on which he has also written a book.

The concept is about breaking our thinking patterns. As we know, thoughts are also habits. We often think only in terms of linear growth—where our lives improve little by little as time moves forward. We think of getting a raise. Or a slightly better car. We think of moving ahead in our career—becoming a senior manager after being a manager.

All through our lives, we are taught to think in a linear fashion. Even the way our friendships and relationships progress is linear. Hence, our lives grow at a steady pace. I know you are interested in growth in all areas of your life, which is why you have picked up this book. I know you are working on improving your life day by day.

But what if you could grow much faster? What if you could change your thinking and go from linear growth to exponential growth? What if your growth didn't just steadily increase but multiplied?

As your Habit Coach, I want to see you live your fullest, biggest and best life. And this begins by changing your thinking. Your mindset has to shift dramatically for this to work. So, look at your life and ask yourself: How can I make this ten times better?

How can I make my financial health ten times better? How can I make my relationships, my lifestyle and my daily habits ten times better? If I read three books a year, how can I start reading thirty books a year?

When you get into the habit of asking yourself these questions, your mindset starts to change. It starts looking for opportunities that could lead to exponential growth instead of opportunities that will lead to linear growth.

Don't just stay focused on the material growth of your life. Think about relationships, knowledge, travel and anything else that holds deep meaning for you. Think of exponential growth in all these aspects of your life. It all begins in your mind.

So, your super simple habit to grow by 10x starts by asking the question: how can I increase this by 10x? What needs to change in my life? What do I need to start doing? What do I need to stop doing?

I can't wait to see you grow by 10x!

Exercise

Identify different aspects of your life where you would like exponential growth.

Pick one that is the most meaningful to you at this stage of your life. Circle it.

Next, write down what 10x growth would look like in this aspect of life. For example, if it's travelling, and you currently take one domestic vacation a year, then 10x growth could mean visiting five new countries in the coming year and quick trips to nearby destinations every six weeks.

Write three habits you will change in order for these goals to become your reality.

Revisit this list every day. Soon your mind will start the magic of working wonders and making these your reality.

Increase Your Self-worth

Did you know that Buckingham Palace is the most expensive home in the world? It is valued at 1.17 billion pounds. It has 775 rooms, including 188 staff rooms, 52 royal and guest bedrooms, 78 bathrooms and 92 offices!

I can only imagine what must have gone through the mind of the person trying to do a valuation of this beautiful home. However, more than the physical property itself, and the obscene number of rooms, offices and so on, its value emanates from its historical nature. It is the home of British royalty, a repository of their family history, a place steeped in the past and simmering with conspiracies and secrets.

Now, most of us have no hope of ever owning a 1.17 billion pound home. But let's understand a few principles. What makes a house worth more? What increases its value? The first thing is the price of the land itself. Depending on how desirable the land is, the price increases. Very often we believe that we have no control over this aspect. But actually, it's very possible to make land covetable. Just look at Dubai—worthless land that was transformed over the years into one of the most expensive real estates in the world. On land that would have been considered dead, the sheikhs added value and transformed it into something desirable.

Next comes the foundation of the property. A deep and strong foundation is essential for a property to last long. Finally, the structure. The aesthetics and the value added by design, contribute to making the property more desirable. Then the amenities add more value, finally leading to a property that is worth a lot more than the land that originally existed.

I get a lot of questions from people about increasing one's self-worth. The way we think of value addition for property is the perfect way to begin thinking about self-worth too.

Where and to whom you are born is the land that already exists. Your roll of the dice with your parents' DNA is completely out of your control. But everything after that is all you. Just like Dubai, you have the ability to add value to what was given to you. To enhance and make more of it. The food you eat and the exercise you do all add to your life.

You then work on your foundation, on the habits that keep you strong and disciplined, that teach you the value of consistency. Focus on six things to make your foundation strong: nutrition, exercise, sleep, de-stressing, hydration and breathing. The quality of your life is based on these principles; start here.

With a strong foundation, you can begin constructing a beautiful life. A life where you add so much value that it becomes insanely desirable. Let me give you a few examples of this.

Pick up a hobby. It might not be obvious, but every new skill is valuable. I remember this boy in college who learnt to play the guitar. All the girls wanted to be around him because he would play the guitar during breaks and would sing so well. He became one of the most popular students around.

Work on your intelligence and knowledge. Add value to people's lives with what you know and how you share it. For example, whatever you are learning from this book can be used to add value to people's lives, if you share with others what you have learnt. Value can come in the form of material things as well. Like the friend who has a car and drops everyone home, or a friend who has a cool house and hosts all the parties.

The point of this chapter is not to force you to do any of this. The point is to make you realise that what you have currently is just the starting point. In order to increase your sense of self-worth, you have to keep adding value to your life. Be on the lookout for ways to add more value. Value comes from the things you, as well as others, desire.

Like it or not, almost all of us evaluate ourselves on how others see us. And so, one needs to keep adding value to one's life. Slowly, it will lead to you feeling more confident. That confidence itself is incredibly desirable and others will want to be around you.

Your super simple habit to increase your self-worth starts by working on the foundation of your life. Work on the six areas I have mentioned to strengthen your foundation. Then, you add value to your life by incorporating skills, hobbies, things, jobs, relationships and so on. The more value you add, the more confidence you will gain and the higher your self-worth will be.

As your habit coach, I want you to have an awesome life. And to have such a life, you need to start adding value to it, little by little.

Exercise

Write down one habit you want to inculcate in each of the six areas mentioned in the chapter.

Nutrition: _____

Exercise: _____

Sleep: _____

De-stressing: _____

Hydration: _____

Breathing: _____

These habits form your foundation. Make sure to make them strong.

Next, think of one hobby and one skill you want to develop to add value to yourself.

Skill: _____

Hobby: _____

These are the embellishments that increase your worth in your mind and in the mind of others.

Form the right habits that help you upskill.

Lastly, figure out a 15-minute slot in the day and keep it exclusively for learning.

Write down when and how you plan to make this habit work. For example: I will read a non-fiction self-help book for 15 minutes in the morning.

_____

_____

_____

Revisit this list every day and remind yourself of your goals and habits. Imprint them in your mind, take the right actions and soon they will be part of your reality.

Radical Ownership

I have an interesting fact to share. Did you know that there was a property in Manhattan that was once owned by five different countries? This house with an area of 20,000 square feet was modelled after the palace of Versailles. It was bought by the Republic of Yugoslavia as their New York embassy in 1946.

But then the republic dissolved into separate countries in 1992 and this is how five countries ended up owning this gorgeous embassy. The five countries were Bosnia, Croatia, Macedonia, Serbia and Slovenia. They settled the ownership of the embassy by selling the property in 2018.

I can't even begin to imagine how complicated that deal must have been due to the involvement of multiple parties. We have similar issues on a smaller scale here in India where parental property gets divided between multiple offsprings and the siblings may take a stance that may make the situation complicated.

This chapter, however, is about a different kind of ownership. It is an idea that comes from the Stoic philosophers. It is a habit that is used to get out of the victim mentality that we often find ourselves in, and to avoid any sort of blame game that we may otherwise engage in due to the lack of control we feel in our lives.

Let's first understand what victim mentality is. It is the feeling that the world is against you. That things are not happening your way. That only bad things keep happening to you. People with victim mentality look at life and think that they are helpless. They keep saying: What can I do about this? The key here is that a person like this does not take responsibility for the things taking place around them. They have resentment towards things in life. They are constantly bitter towards the world around them. Being around such people is no fun because you will get blamed for everything.

Another common thought process for such people is: What did I do to deserve this? The feeling that the world owes you something, that you are not getting what you deserve, is common among such people. They forget that the world owes them nothing.

The aspect of these people that troubles me the most is that they will grumble and complain about their problems. But if you offer them a solution, they will have a longer list of why it will not work. For every solution you offer, they will have five more problems. As your habit coach, I want you to never get stuck in this trap of being a victim.

The Stoics believed in something that I call radical ownership. It is the belief that you are in control of everything that is happening everywhere in the world. If there is a war happening between five countries at the opposite end of the globe, you are still in control of it.

This belief of being in control makes you the owner of what is happening around you. Since you are now the owner of the problem, you can no longer play the victim.

As the owner of the problem, you have two choices. You can choose to do something about it or you can choose to not do anything about it. Using this approach, you change your thinking completely. You no longer feel like you do not have control.

The reason why I call this radical ownership is that it makes you feel you have ownership over everything. And hence if something happening anywhere in the world affects you, you have a choice to do something about it.

For example, you can choose to protest the war taking place at the other end of the world. Or you can choose to make better choices with regard to the plastics you use. If the war is of no concern to you, you can choose not to do anything about it. Or you can choose not to worry about plastic and instead focus on something else.

If someone is being mean to you or causing problems for you, you can choose to fight back, punch them, call the cops, or you can choose to do nothing. With radical ownership, the choice is always yours.

So, your simple habit starts by realising that everything you do is a choice. That you are in control of everything that is taking place in the world around you.

You can no longer blame anyone else for anything. Everything is your choice.

When you start thinking like this, the victim inside you disappears. You are now in control.

Exercise

Reflect on an instance or a period in your life where you had planned for something and it didn't go as you had thought it would. Think about how it made you feel. Now, think of why you felt that way and write down the reasons below.

_____
_____
_____

Take a look at these reasons and see if there is an underlying thread of blame that you can spot. Is there a feeling of powerlessness? At any point in time, did you feel like a victim of situations? If you answered 'yes' to any of these questions, then this is the right time to adopt radical ownership.

Read the chapter again and give it another try. This time, take radical ownership of the situation and write down possible choices you had back then.

Remember, you always have a choice. You have control over everything. You can choose to try again, you can choose to do things differently, you can choose to do nothing, and/or most importantly you can choose to feel a certain way about the whole thing.

Mention choices you had back then—and choices you have now—about how you could have done or thought differently about a situation that went out of your control.

Create vs Compete

Have you noticed that I love digging into the etymology of words? It's because the origin of a word gives us a true sense of what it means. In today's day and age, we often use words in diluted forms, where the essence is missing.

Did you know that the word 'create' comes from the Latin word 'creatus'? The Latin original means to bring into being, to make out of thin air, to make something grow.

We look at creativity as something colourful, funky and cool. People smoking up and dreaming up something. When I talk to people they often say that they are not creative only because they do not want to associate with that stereotype. But the word or the act of creation is something completely different. And it is beautiful.

In today's fast-paced world, we are taught another word early on: competition. Right from our school life, we start competing. Whether it is in class for grades or in the track and field events for medals. Later in life, we compete for a job. And then we compete with our co-workers. Once we become the head of a company or run our own business, we start competing with other businesses. If we are homemakers, we compete with the parents of our children's friends. In a word, for most of us, competition is an integral part of our lives. It is a treadmill we are running on. One competition to the next.

The problem with competition is that it teaches and gives us a scarcity mindset. It makes us believe that there is a scarcity of resources—a scarcity of money, property or talent—and that is what we all are fighting for. I realised that most of the companies I worked with operated from this position of fear. They were scared of losing. And hence they were too afraid to grow. They just wanted to compete.

As your habit coach I want you to realise that competing is nothing but following the herd and hoping to be better than the others. It becomes about being better in relative terms rather than being good in absolute terms. And that is why I want you to get into the habit of creating and not competing. When you create something you do this from a position of power. You step away from the herd and forge a path for yourself. Creating is where growth and the magic happen. But creating is scary as it is uncharted.

When I quit my family business and the safety net it gave me, I was scared. I could have easily done life coaching or something similar that already existed. I could have charged my clients less than others and undercut the competition. Instead, I decided to create a new category of coaching called habit coaching. When I started, the concept of habit coaching did not exist. Googling 'Habit Coach' got you zero results. Instead, it showed you a book titled *The Coaching Habit*, which has nothing to do with habit coaching.

I created this category and hence could trademark Habit Coach. It was scary and exhilarating. Now there are so many people calling themselves habit coaches, after seeing my success. But they are trying to compete and not create.

Another example from my life is my podcast. I decided to create a podcast and give away all my knowledge for free. So many people told me it was the worst idea they had ever heard! They told me how everyone would copy my ideas or steal my work.

And I told all these well-wishers, that I was fine with letting people steal my ideas and my work. They will just be competing. They will never have a fresh idea of their own because they believe that ideas are scarce resources. But clearly, that's not the case. You only need to learn how to create them.

I use these examples because I want to show you that it is possible. It is possible to win without competing. Another reason for sharing these examples is because I am very proud of these achievements. So, this is a little pat on my back as well.

One of the things I learnt on this journey is to be yourself. Because when you are yourself, you are unique and whatever you do will be different from what others have done or are doing and hence it will be rooted in creation. If you try to please others, you will change yourself and hence fall into the competition trap.

So, your simple habit starts by learning the power of creation. To adopt the habit of constantly creating—at home, at work, anywhere and everyone.

Exercise

For this exercise, list three passions you had when you were younger.

_____
_____
_____

Now that you've put it in writing, pick any one passion. Bring your unique skill to grow that passion through your work. The objective is to enjoy your creation and go through the creation process. Nurture the creative instinct in you.

Write down one goal that you will achieve through this passion. For example, if music is your chosen passion, your goal could be as simple as learning to play a certain song on your chosen instrument.

_____
_____
_____

Next, in your education or work life, choose a project or a problem that is close to your heart. For a minute, do not think of your peers or any existing solutions. Imagine you have no limitations. How will you make the situation better? What if you had all the power to create a unique solution. What would you do?

_____
_____
_____

Whenever you are faced with a situation, ask yourself, how could you add value by using the creative genius within you. By being your powerful self. Leave the competition and herd behind.

Persistence

I am sure you are familiar with the classic nursery rhyme, 'Itsy-Bitsy Spider'. But did you know it was made for adults? *Camp and Camino in Lower California*, which was published in 1910, included the poem, except, in it, it wasn't an itsy-bitsy spider that was climbing up the water spout. It was a 'Blooming Bloody Spider' that was climbing up a spider web.

The author had written the poem as a cry for the working classes in America at the time, to not lose hope and continue to crawl up the web. The web being the American dream of success. It was a poem to incite societal change! And somewhere along the way, someone clearly broke multiple copyright laws and turned this poem for adults into a poem for children.

When I was in school, not only was I taught the English version of the poem, I was made to learn the Hindi version as well, where we had an itsy-bitsy makoda! The poem was used to teach us two things: hard work and a never-give-up attitude.

Today, the itsy-bitsy spider story can be encapsulated in one word meant for adults: persistence.

Persistence is the ability to pick yourself up after you have been knocked down. It is the ability to keep getting up after being knocked down many times over. Persistence is that inner belief in what you are doing and a belief that you will get there no matter what. Persistence is the key to unlocking your dreams.

If you feel unsuccessful right now take a look at your life and ask yourself if you were persistent in your efforts towards your goal. Did you give up at the first sign of trouble? Did you throw your hands up in the air and quit when things got hard?

The truth is that most of us never get up after being knocked down. We move to the sidelines of life and prefer to watch instead of being part of the action. When you read about the great people in society, you read about their persistence. You read about how they kept getting up, after being beaten down by life. They kept getting up even after there seemed no hope for a future.

If there is one thing that I have learnt through reading about these great humans, it is that they had made persistence a habit. It was something that they practised every single day. They had a sharp clarity of purpose and they let nothing come in their way.

With that kind of persistence, there is no way they could have not succeeded.

One of my favourite quotes from the book *Think and Grow Rich* by Napoleon Hill is: 'Those who have cultivated the habit of persistence seem to enjoy insurance against failure.'

Isn't that powerful?

As your habit coach, I want you to cultivate this habit of persistence. Don't just quit at the first sight of failure. Keep getting up and keep moving ahead.

In my life too, persistence is what helps me succeed. When we first launched a phone app, it failed. We had spent a lot of money and time on it. It was heartbreaking. But we learnt from our mistakes and tried again. The goal now was to add tremendous value by getting all the content I produce every day in one place. To actually show and teach people how to form habits, step by step.

I haven't given up and I am focused on making this app a tremendous success. Just like itsy-bitsy spider climbing up the water spout!

So, your super simple habit starts by having a direction in which you want your life to head. Be clear about this. Then learn how to get up after each fall. Learn from the fall. Figure out what went wrong, fix the issue and try again.

Persistence is your insurance against failure.

And, of course, do get to the Playstore and check out the app. It is called Awesome180.

Exercise

For this exercise, identify a goal that you've been thinking about for a while. That one desire that you have not been able to fulfil.

Write down why it is important to you.

Next, mention why you haven't been able to accomplish the goal so far. When did you attempt it last and what were your learnings?

Promise yourself that you will continue pursuing the goal even if you face challenges this time. Write down any two actions that you will do if a setback appears.

Also, write down three challenging things you have done where you failed in the beginning but persisted and achieved your target in the end.

Read this whenever you face challenges, to remind yourself that it's only a slip, not a fall!

Stop Worrying

Did you know that the word 'worry' comes from the Old English word 'wyrgan'? Wyrgan meant to wrap around the neck and strangle. Then in Middle English, the original verb changed its meaning. Now it meant to 'seize by the throat and tear'. Just like a wolf biting your neck and tearing it apart.

Later it began to mean to figuratively 'harass'. Like a mother shouting at her eldest son, 'Stop worrying your baby brother.' Only in the nineteenth century did it begin to mean to 'cause anxiety'. For instance, 'I am worried about my father's health.' This is the meaning we all associate with the word 'worry' today.

I always find the origin of words interesting. Imagine, 'worry' meant to be seized by the throat and have it ripped out. I know that very often when we worry, it feels like our throats are being ripped out. It's that feeling of fear and dread, all rolled into one. We are unable to speak and are frozen in terror.

In fact, this is exactly what worry does. It prevents us from taking action. It prevents us from making decisions and moving forward. Instead, we see the worst possible outcome and let it marinate in our minds. It steeps, like tea leaves in a pot of hot water, getting stronger and stronger, darker and darker. Until it is too bitter to swallow.

This has been a reality for us over the last few years. All sorts of worries have emerged in our lives. From financial worries to those about our health. All the air pollution that has become a part of modern-day cities makes one worry about breathing itself! I have seen people completely debilitated by worrying about things. Two words that are used most when worrying about something: What if? These two words have killed so many dreams and laid so many opportunities to waste. What if this happens, what if that happens? It is the mind playing games. Dreaming up scenarios that do not exist. Predicting a future that cannot be predicted.

I used to worry a lot. My mind used to be like a storm: agitated, dark and noisy. There was no peace. I would just keep worrying about the future. And I would freeze with those thoughts so much that I would take no action. My work suffered and so did my relationships.

That's when I came upon a flow chart. I do not know who invented it. But it is a popular flow chart and you might have seen it as well. It's very simple.

It starts by asking a question: 'Do you have a problem?' If the answer is no, then it leads you to 'Don't worry'. It makes us realise that half our problems are a product of our imagination.

On the other hand, if your answer to 'Do you have a problem?' is yes, then the flow chart takes you to the next question: 'Can you do something about it?' If the answer to this is yes, you know how to solve the problem and then when you have no problem left, the flow chart will lead you back to 'Don't worry'. If you cannot do anything about the problem you have, then it leads you back to 'Don't worry'. After all, you will not achieve anything by worrying if you have no control over the problem.

This is the key to living well. There is never a reason to worry. If you take action and solve the problem, there is no more reason to worry. And if you can't do anything about a problem, stop worrying and instead be open to being entertained or amused by what is to follow.

Ever since I got into the habit of using this flow chart, my problems have disappeared. This is because half the time there was no real problem and even when there was one, it wasn't as bad as my worrying made it out to be!

So, your simple habit starts by imprinting this flow chart on your mind and using it every time you find yourself faced with a problem. Soon, you'll find yourself letting certain situations take their own course.

Don't let the tea leaves remain in the hot water. Remove them from the pot and enjoy your tea!

Exercise

Write down some of the things you are worried about.

_____
_____
_____

Can you take any actions that will cause the worry to evaporate?

Write down the action below. Go, do it NOW.

_____
_____
_____

If there is no action you can take to improve the situation, why worry? Instead, write a pledge that you will let go of worrying and look forward to whatever unfolds.

_____
_____
_____

_____

Remember this every time you see yourself worrying about a problem.

_____

Curiosity

Did you know that Christopher Columbus may not have been the first European to sail to North America? Apparently, a Norse explorer, Leif Erikson had sailed and discovered a sea route to America way back in 1000 AD. According to the Norse sagas, Erikson established a settlement in what they called Vinland. This was around Newfoundland in Canada. And, according to carbon dating, the settlement existed there for quite a while. What I found interesting is that Erikson's father was Erik the Red, a very famous Norseman who had established the Norse settlement in Greenland. So clearly, exploring ran in his blood.

Recently, I have been watching a lot of Viking shows on Netflix. I found their portrayal of exploring quite amazing. You get in a little boat and sail off to discover a new world. You set off not knowing what you will find. That sense of adventure and the unknown is missing in our lives today. Nowadays, we want to see the proof before we explore. Prove it to me and then I will think about it.

I recognised this while talking to a friend. We were discussing something about spirituality, and she said that it needs to be proven before she can consider exploring it.

I did some research and learnt that this style of thinking is born from science. Our society today is built on the basis of science and hence this style of thinking has seeped into our everyday language. If it can't be proven, it does not exist. If it can't be repeated as an experiment, it is faulty.

I also think exactly like that. I want to see the science behind all the changes I make in my life as well. I want to see the science behind the habits I share with you on my podcast.

But there are times when there is no proof. There are times when you have to put on your little explorer hat and then just dive in. Like those brave Norseman sailing out into the sea, not knowing what they will find. It is this spirit of exploring that helps us achieve new things in life. If we do not explore, we become stagnant. We remain the same. And in a world that is growing, when we remain the same, we are technically moving backwards.

As your habit coach, I want to ask you, when was the last time you did something new? When did you last go exploring, not knowing where it will lead you and what you will find?

A great habit to start you off as an explorer is to wonder about things. What I like to do is have a questioning expression and rub my chin while I wonder. It just adds to the drama of it all!

I wonder what this new dish on the restaurant's menu is like?

I wonder if there is a different route I can take to the office?

I wonder what I will learn from this new online course?

So, your super simple habit to become an explorer and seek out new things in life starts with simply wondering. Get into the habit of saying *I wonder what*, or *I wonder who*, and so on. Bring out your inner explorer and watch your life expand as the known world did at the hands of the Norse explorers.

I can almost visualise Leif Erikson standing at the shore, looking out at the sea and saying, 'I wonder' or probably more accurately, in Norwegian, 'Jeg lurer' (pronounced 'yaie lur e').

Exercise

For this exercise, bring out your 'explorer hat'. Seriously.
Go get that hat or cap languishing in your cupboard.
From this day on, the hat will be a part of your study
or workspace. Whenever you see that hat, wear it for
a few minutes and say the words, 'I wonder.' Now the
rule is, once you say the words, 'I wonder,' you need
to think and finish the sentence with a question that
comes to your mind.

As you keep doing this, make a note of your 'I wonder'
questions below.

_____

Make this a habit and soon you will start seeing the
world very differently. You will be asking interesting
questions about things and your thinking will change.
The trick here is to make your brain switch on its
'curious mode', by using an external prop. We forget
to be curious in our daily, busy lives. It's time to change
that!

_____

Pigeon Nest

Let me tell you about flying rats. Did you know that pigeons never nest in trees? I realised this when I was at my farm during the lockdown. I stayed there for eight months and not once did I see a pigeon.

We are so used to seeing pigeons in the city that we take it for granted that they are everywhere. They are normally called rats with wings or flying rats just because they are so plentiful in cities. And the reason they are so plentiful in cities is that they are rock nesters. This means that in the wild they would normally nest in cliffs or mountain ledges. Pigeons will look for little holes high up in cliffs and build a nest.

The male will find a good spot for a nest and start cooing. Once he finds a mate, he will build a nest in the cliffs. In the cities, our buildings act like cliff spaces. They offer the birds lots of little nooks and crannies to nest in. Our cities are paradise for pigeons to thrive in.

In the same way, we humans too are creatures of habit. Some like spending time in libraries, some at work, others like shopping in the malls, while some like getting drunk in a bar.

But unlike pigeons that will never nest in trees, we have the ability to make a conscious decision. We are able to choose what we want to do, where we want to be, how we want to show up in the world.

Every now and then, we feel stuck. Where we are now in life is not where we want to be. However, all our old habits are keeping us trapped in this same space. But more importantly, all the people in our lives are also keeping us in the same place. You see, all the pigeons nest together. All the eagles nest in the trees.

When you want to change your life, your habits, your environment, the people you spend time with will have to change.

I remember when I wanted to stop being overweight and unhealthy. I had to stop meeting friends who would eat dinners at eleven in the night and then drink and party till 4 a.m. I had to change that environment to ensure I could change my habits.

Soon I started to spend more time in different kinds of gyms in the city. I signed up for yoga classes and spent time at yoga studios. I met yoga teachers who would eat at 6 p.m. and be asleep by 10 p.m. Pizza restaurants got replaced by salad bars. Long island iced teas got replaced by Kombucha.

The gist of all this is that it is important where we spend our time. Our environment decides who we will become.

Many of us are stuck in toxic environments at home. We spend as much time as possible outside, in a new environment. Many of us want to be rich and wealthy but are stuck in an environment where we are not allowed to feel rich and wealthy.

I remember Aristotle Onassis, once the richest man in the world, saying that he would advise people to spend time in the fanciest hotel in the city. Just sit in the lobby. Or in the coffee shop and order the cheapest thing on the menu. But spend time in that location. You will start to pick up things from observing the people around you. You will begin to form the mindset.

You might make friends sitting in that lobby. Those friends might make you meet other people. And soon you will have a different social group. The places where we choose to spend our time play a big role in the kind of life we want to create for ourselves.

So, your super simple habit starts by figuring out what kind of life you want to live. Then figure out where other people, whose life you find attractive, spend their time. Go and change your location.

Like I said earlier, you are not a pigeon, you have the ability to move and change where you nest!

Exercise

Write down three important changes that you want to make in order to live your dream life.

_____

_____

_____

Next, write down who you have to become in the future to inhabit your dream life.

What would your daily routine look like?

_____

_____

_____

Analyse the gap between your today and a day in your dream life.

Think about how you can bridge that gap and write down the answers to these questions.

Who should you surround yourself with? What are the important location changes that you have to make? What are the daily habits you will have to change?

_____

_____

_____

Be Bold

Did you know that one of the first interracial kisses on American television was on *Star Trek*? It was between Captain Kirk and Uhura. Originally, the kiss was going to be between Spock and Uhura, but William Shatner jumped in when he realised that he would be making history.

If you are not familiar with *Star Trek*, it is a cult superhit TV show, where the crew of the Star Ship Enterprise have a mission to travel to the edge of the known universe and discover new worlds. The show is famous for its opening lines: *Space: the final frontier. These are the voyages of the Starship Enterprise. Its five-year mission: to explore strange new worlds. To seek out new life and new civilisations. To boldly go where no man has gone before!*

The word 'boldly' is what stood out for me. It is such a strong and powerful word. As a child, I must have said these opening lines a thousand times while watching the show. But it is only now that I realise just how powerful the word 'boldly' is. There is a sense of heft to it. A sense of class. A sense of overcoming fear. Standing up for your beliefs and for what is right and just in the world.

The dictionary defines the word 'bold' as (of a person, action or idea) showing a willingness to take risks; confident and courageous. This got me thinking. Can being bold be a habit? Can it eventually become a part of our personality, a part of who we are?

For many of us, being confident is just a dream. We are filled with self-doubt. We visualise the worst of ourselves. We do not have confidence in our abilities to do things. As a consequence of this lack of confidence, we don't do anything. We pass on the opportunities that life gives us. We squander the riches that could have been ours.

The next word used to describe being bold is 'courage'. Courage is simply the ability to control fear in uncomfortable or dangerous situations. In our lives, we hardly encounter any dangerous situations. But we do often find ourselves in uncomfortable situations. And we have become frightened of being uncomfortable. We get offended too easily. We give up without trying too hard. We have lost the ability to do uncomfortable things.

Imagine how different our lives would be, if only we were more confident and courageous. In other words, if only we were bold!

Recently, I was invited to be on prime-time television. A news channel had invited me to discuss financial habits. Now, for most of us, this can be scary. It wasn't any different for me. However, the real kicker here was that the whole interview would be in Hindi.

To put things in perspective, I had failed almost every single Hindi exam in my life. My elocution skills were non-existent.

So, when I was offered to be interviewed in Hindi, what did I do? I said yes before my brain could process the fear.

Being on a very popular news channel in Hindi ... AAAh! I was scared and nervous. But I remembered the word 'bold'. And this was me practising my habit of being bold. I was not confident in my Hindi skills. But I was confident in my communication skills. I knew that I could get my point across even though my grammar would be all over the place.

The courage came from knowing that there was no real danger here. It would definitely be uncomfortable, but that could be dealt with. When the day and time came, I shared the financial habits that I thought would help most people. I focused on helping others and not on how others would see me.

The interview went very well. The anchor, Kavita, did a fabulous job jumping in and helping when I needed it. You can watch the interview if you like. Just search for Ashdin Doctor ET NOW.

So, your super simple habit starts by observing the times and events in your life that require you to be bold. It could be standing up to someone. Or getting out of a toxic relationship. Or taking up a new job.

Start small and work on becoming bolder and bolder. Fearless, confident and courageous! Just like the journeys of the Starship Enterprise. Boldly go where no one has gone before.

And yes, for all you fellow *Star Trek* geeks out there, I boldly changed that last line.

Exercise

Being bold is an essential habit. To make it a part of your personality, do this exercise.

Write down three things you would do, if you were being bold today. This can be attempting a hobby that you are afraid to try. It may be standing up to someone who is not nice to you. It may be taking a small risk in your career. It can even be a new hairstyle you've wanted but been too uncertain to try.

Next, describe your fear. What is it that you are afraid of? What is stopping you from doing what you want?

Now analyse if it's truly dangerous or merely uncomfortable. Visualise yourself putting all your imagined fears in a box, filling it with cement, and throwing it into a deep ocean. Those fears can't reach you anymore.

Go back to the first answer, and pick any one of the three. Take an action, however small it may be. As you complete that action, acknowledge your courage. Believe in your bold self and feel the power and strength that comes with being bold. Appreciate your effort and gently nudge yourself to start with the next two on the list.

Stop Whining

Did you know that whining is one of the most annoying sounds on the planet? In a study conducted by researchers, people rated the whining of children as a bigger distraction than nails on a chalkboard, heavy drilling noise, crying and the screeching of wood!

Kids begin their whiny behaviour between the ages of two and four. They realise that this tone of voice gets a reaction from the adults. It is their way of communicating and getting some form of power. It works because parents respond with frustration and anger. The pitch of the sound made while whining makes it even more annoying than crying.

Since whining seems to get people's attention, many people continue whining into adulthood. We all know people who whine on and drone on in that annoying pitch. You feel like hitting them on the head with something!

The difference between adults and kids whining is that kids whine about things that they want immediately. They ask for it upfront: 'I want chocolate now!' Adults, on the other hand, manage to sneak whining into a perfectly normal conversation: 'So, Susie, what fun things are you doing this weekend?' And

Susie replies, 'Oh, you know, between work and the kids and bills to pay, what life do I have! I am so busy I can't do anything fun.'

That, my friends, is a case of an adult whining. It is an adult's call for attention, a way to get people to notice them. There are three typical reasons for an adult to whine:

They are deeply distressed by something and feel powerless to change it.

They feel simultaneously angry and sad about the situation and worry that it is their own fault.

They do not know how to soothe themselves.

As adults, we start whining when we find ourselves in any of these positions, and we whine to anyone and everyone who will listen to us. We don't realise that, eventually, that person is going to get fed up and stop talking to us. And that will only further add to our woes. Now, before trying to change the world, we have to first change ourselves. So, let's see what we can do to stop whining.

First, notice the tone of your voice. Is it nasal, high-pitched? Are you using single words like 'Please! Now!' instead of full sentences?

Next, be aware of your facial expressions. Are you smiling or frowning? Try smiling and looking up while asking for things. This way it doesn't seem like whining or complaining.

Then, notice how you frame your sentences: 'I love you so much but you don't spend enough time with me. I am always asking you to meet me.' That was whining and complaining. Instead, say: 'I love you and it would be amazing to spend more time with each other! No amount of time seems like it's enough with you.' Did you see the difference? The first is complaining; the second is suggesting and complimenting.

Which of these would get a better response? The whining would get you the attention but ultimately, a negative result. The other might get you a dinner date!

The next thing that is so destructive about whiners is that they try guilt-tripping you into action. They try to make you feel guilty for not doing something. We need to understand that using guilt is a form of aggression. This is because the other person feels attacked every time you use it! If you do this all the time, people will stop wanting to work with you or be around you.

Now that you know what to look for, your super-simple habit to stop whining starts by identifying the things that make you whine.

All of us have something or the other that makes us whine. Not spending enough time with someone, not having enough money, hating your job, not feeling loved, and so on.

The next step is to start working on yourself. When you catch yourself whining, try reframing that sentence with a compliment. Try saying the same thing with a smile. Try reframing the idea or thought.

If you do whine, move on. Don't be like a toddler or a whiny baby! Be a strong powerful adult—one who makes conversation, not annoying whining noises.

Exercise

For this exercise observe your behaviour to know if you have the habit of whining. This is how you can do it.

Notice how you respond to people when they ask you how you are doing. Lookout for your choice of words, tone and the feeling you are trying to communicate.

If you catch yourself whining, ask yourself, 'Why do I feel the need to whine?'

For example, are you trying to gain sympathy? Are you trying to protect someone? Do you need attention?

Whatever the reason may be, note it down.

_____
_____
_____

Next, reframe your thoughts. To reverse this habit of whining, you need to cultivate the habit of gratitude.

Every time you catch yourself whining, replace that with at least three unique things that you are grateful for. This will bring you back to your present moment. Write down three things you are grateful for.

_____
_____
_____

Follow these simple changes and soon whining will be a thing of the past!